Urban Prospects

JOHN WOLFORTH
Faculty of Education
University of British Columbia

ROGER LEIGH
Department of Geography
University of British Columbia

MCCLELLAND AND STEWART LIMITED

The Canadian Publishers
McClelland and Stewart Limited
25 Hollinger Road, Toronto 374

Printed and bound in Canada

Contents

List of Illustrations

Preface

This book is called *Urban Prospects*. The word "prospect" has at least two meanings. It can mean "an extensive view of a scene or landscape," and it can mean "an expectation of the future." As applied to cities, in this book, both meanings are appropriate. We intend to take an extensive look at the nature of cities and especially Canadian cities. We hope to arrive at an increased understanding of the reasons for the recent rapid growth of Canadian cities, to know more about the functions of particular cities, about the internal form of cities, and about how people live in cities, and to appreciate the problems of the complicated cities of today. Then we hope to be able to look forward to the cities that may be in store for us in the future, in which many of us will spend the rest of our adult lives and our old age. Will our urban problems get worse, or are they solvable? Are our cities out of control or can we plan the kind of cities we want? Can we create more efficient, attractive, and livable cities for ourselves and our children? These are important questions for all concerned citizens, but we must undertake an "extensive view" of the present situation, and understand its nature and origins, before we can raise these "expectations of the future" in a sensible way.

The word "prospect" is also connected with the word "prospector," one who explores a region for minerals. We are also prospectors, prospectors of the urban environments in which we live. Old-time prospectors sometimes found gold. We shall find something more important—understanding of our society and of ourselves.

J. W. and R. L.

ONE

The City Scene

1. Introduction

More people throughout the world are living in towns and cities than ever before. One hundred years ago, Canada was a predominantly rural country. Today, eighty out of every one hundred Canadians live in an urban centre, and more than twenty of every hundred live in one of the three major urban centres of Montreal, Toronto, and Vancouver. In this book we shall look at some of the causes and the consequences of this movement and examine the nature of the cities we have created and which for most of us have become the home environment.

The study of *urbanization,* or the movement of people into towns and cities, is important for a number of reasons. Even those of us who do not live in urban centres are very strongly influenced by them. We go into town for school, shopping, the movies, or even just for a little excitement. Our TV and radio stations are in towns, as are our libraries, museums and art galleries, and the offices of our major businesses and of our governments. In short, we live in an *urban society,* in which the majority of people, activities, and institutions are found in cities. An urban society has always been regarded as a rather special form of human community, offering special opportunities to its members. For example, the very word "civilization" comes from the Latin word *civis,* meaning the citizen of a town or city, and for us, as for the Romans, much of what we call civilization seems to be associated in some way with cities.

Because of all this, and especially because of the recency of large-scale urbanization, many of our attitudes are quite different even from those of our grandparents, who in all probability grew up in rural areas. For example, they had to face problems of living on isolated farms or in small villages where everyone knew everyone else. Most of us, on the other hand, have to face problems of living in towns and cities where it is all too easy to get lost in the crowd. They never knew the problems we experience daily of urban noise, air and water pollution, traffic and so on. Since the pace of urbanization seems to be increasing these problems are likely to become even greater in the future.

2.   Urbanization in Canada

The following table shows the percentages of Canada's population living in urban centres between 1851 and 1961.

Table 1-1   Percentages of Canada's population living in urban centres, 1851-1961

Canada or province[1]	1851	1861	1871	1881	1891	1901
Canada (incl. Newfoundland)	—	—	—	—	—	—
Canada (excl. Newfoundland)	13.1	15.8	18.3	23.3	29.8	34.9
Newfoundland	—	—	—	—	—	—
Maritimes	9.0	9.9	11.9	15.3	18.8	24.5
Prince Edward Island	—	9.3	9.4	10.5	13.1	14.5
Nova Scotia	7.5	7.6	8.3	14.7	19.4	27.7
New Brunswick	14.0	13.1	17.6	17.6	19.9	23.1
Quebec	14.9	16.6	19.9	23.8	28.6	36.1
Ontario	14.0	18.5	20.6	27.1	35.0	40.3
Prairies	—	—	—	—	—	19.3
Manitoba	—	—	—	14.9	23.3	24.9
Saskatchewan	—	—	—	—	—	6.1
Alberta	—	—	—	—	—	16.2
British Columbia	—	—	9.0	18.3	42.6	46.4

	1911	1921	1931	1941	1951	1961
Canada (incl. Newfoundland)	—	—	—	—	62.4	69.7
Canada (excl. Newfoundland)	41.8	47.4	52.5	55.7	62.9	70.2
Newfoundland	—	—	—	—	43.3	50.7
Maritimes	30.9	38.8	39.7	44.1	47.4	49.5
Prince Edward Island	16.0	18.8	19.5	22.1	25.1	32.4
Nova Scotia	36.7	44.8	46.6	52.0	54.5	54.3
New Brunswick	26.7	35.2	35.4	38.7	42.8	46.5
Quebec	44.5	51.8	59.5	61.2	66.8	74.3
Ontario	49.5	58.8	63.1	67.5	72.5	77.3
Prairies	27.9	28.7	31.3	32.4	44.5	57.6
Manitoba	39.3	41.5	45.2	45.7	56.0	63.9
Saskatchewan	16.1	16.8	20.3	21.3	30.4	43.0
Alberta	29.4	30.7	31.8	31.9	47.6	63.3
British Columbia	50.9	50.9	62.3	64.0	68.6	72.6

SOURCE: Leroy O. Stone, *Urban Development in Canada* (Ottawa: Queen's Printer, 1968), p. 29.

[1]From 1851 to 1911 the urban population figures refer to incorporated cities, towns and villages of 1,000 and over only; from 1921 the percentages are estimates of the percentages which would have been reported in the respective censuses had the 1961 Census definition and procedures been used; for 1961 the figures are those published according to the 1961 Census definition of "urban."

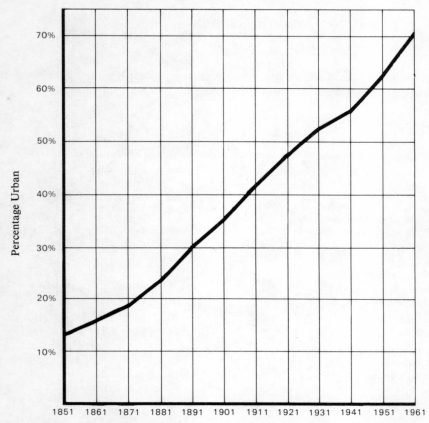

Fig. 1-1 Growth of urban population in Canada (excluding Newfoundland), 1851-1961, expressed as percentages of total population.

1. Figure 1-1 is based on the statistics given in the table, and shows graphically the changes which have occurred in the percentage of Canada's population which is urban. Construct a similar graph showing changes for the Maritimes, Quebec, Ontario, the Prairies, and British Columbia.
2. In which parts of Canada has the pace of urbanization been most rapid? In which parts has it been least rapid? Which regions of Canada have generally been more urbanized?
3. Make three maps of Canada (like that shown in Figure 1-2) for three separate periods, 1851, 1911, and 1961, showing the percentage of urban population in each province. Shade those provinces with less than 55 per cent as urban population in a light shade; those with between 55 and 70 per cent in a medium shade; and those with over 70 per cent in a dark shade.
4. How would you account for the differences shown both by the graphs and by the maps?

Many of the early French and English settlers on Canada's shores were farmers. Poor transportation made it necessary for them to provide for as many of their own needs as possible, so that their farms were almost completely self-sufficient. A settler had to be not just a farmer but a "jack-of-all-trades," for not only did

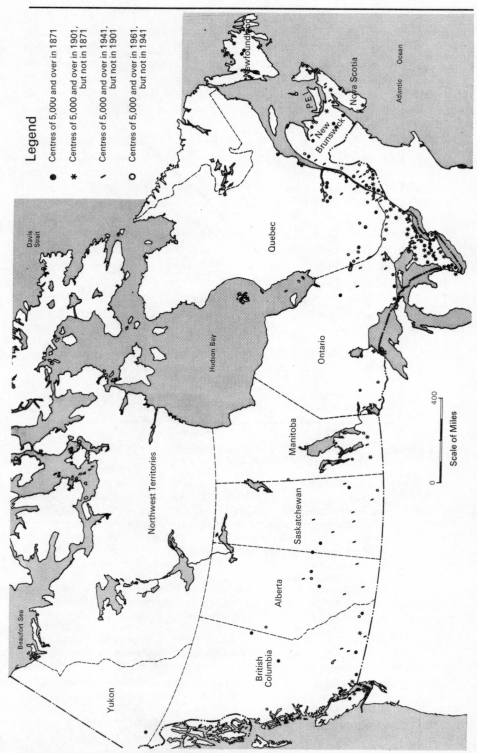

Fig. 1-2 Canadian towns of over 5,000 in population, 1871-1961

he grow raw materials, but he also manufactured them into the commodities needed by himself and his family. Clothing, furniture, tools, and many other things besides food were both produced and consumed on the farm itself. As Canada grew, however, not only were there too many people to be supported by the farms alone, but the growing complexity of life called forth an ever increasing number of specialized occupations. Agriculture itself became more specialized and commercialized, and towns grew up as service centres for the agricultural population, as merchants, blacksmiths, carpenters, and cobblers set up in business at places where their skills would be available to as many potential customers as possible. Administrative and governmental activities were set up in some centres, while other towns began to collect and distribute the products of the increasingly specialized farms to distant markets. Later, some towns became centres for the exploitation of mineral and forest resources, and eventually centres of large-scale factory industry and corporate business.

Thus, the pace of urbanization has increased since Canada's early days. It has also varied from one part of the country to another and still varies today. That is to say, some parts of Canada became more *urbanized* earlier than other parts, and some parts are more urbanized than others today. This is shown not only by your graphs and shaded maps of the provinces, but also by the distribution of towns of over 5,000 in population shown in Figure 1-2.

5. Which parts of Canada became more intensely urbanized first?
6. What advantages might these areas have had which would favour early urbanization?
7. Which parts of Canada now have the greatest number of towns with more than 5,000 people?
8. Refer to a source such as *The Statesman's Yearbook* to find what other countries have the same level of urbanization as modern Canada.

3.   Similarities Among Cities

If you are one of the majority of Canadians who now live in urban centres, it will be possible for you to relate this book very closely to the place where you live, since many of the observations in it apply in a general way to towns and cities across Canada. One of the main purposes of our study is to look for similarities between places and, by examining the places closely, to try to make statements which are true of a large number of cases rather than being true of only one. It is *generalizations* of this kind which enable us to understand something about places we may not even have visited and which reduce mountains of specific observations to a few useful concepts or principles.

All of us use generalizations in everyday life. For example, when we use the word "city" we do not necessarily think of any particular place, but rather of a kind of place with specific characteristics. In knowing that Toronto, Paris, and New York are all cities, you already know quite a lot about them. If you were to visit them, many of their characteristics would not come as a complete surprise. By discussing the following exercise together, you should be able to reach agreement on what some of the common characteristics of cities are.

9. Complete these sentences in as many ways as you can:
   a) "I know that a place is a city when it has . . . . ."
   b) "I know that the place where I live is (or is not) a city because it has . . . . ."

By putting your sentences in different words, you could now make a number of generalizations about cities; for example, "cities have large populations," or "cities have tall buildings at their centres," or "cities are centres of industry and trade." Now we can look at these and at other generalizations, and try to build up a concept of the city which we can use as a basis for further study. Figures 1-3 and 1-4 are views of rural and urban landscapes in Canada.

Fig. 1-3 The rural landscape

10. Which of the generalizations you have made about cities apply to the scene shown in Figure 1-4? Which do not?
11. People have to earn a living whether they are in the city or the countryside. Using the appearance of the buildings and other clues given in Figure 1-4, make a list of some of the jobs which people working in the area may have.
12. Make a similar list for Figure 1-3. What differences are there between your two lists?
13. What further generalizations can you now make about cities?

For example, we may notice from the two photographs that buildings are closer together in the urban than in the rural landscape. We can guess from this that the *density of population,* or the number of people living in a given area of land, is generally higher in cities than it is in the countryside. Of course, the density of population does vary from city to city, or from one part of the city to another. In some Asian cities, population densities are as high as 30,000 people per square mile, but in Canada they are always much lower. Even so, in the central parts of large Canadian cities, many people may make their homes very close together, often in high-rise apartment buildings. Figure 1-5 shows a map of the

Fig. 1-4 The urban landscape

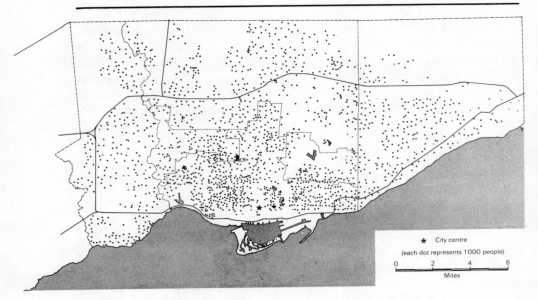

Fig. 1-5 Distribution of residential population in Metropolitan Toronto

distribution of population in Metropolitan Toronto; it shows clearly the high population density and also the varied population density within a large area.

14. Using the scale given in Figure 1-5, draw squares enclosing an area of 4 sq. mi. in several parts of the region, including a location near the centre of the city, a suburban location, and some locations near the edge of the Metropolitan area. Calculate the density of population at each of the places you have chosen. Also, measure the distance from these places to the centre of Toronto. Construct a graph with population density represented on the vertical axis and distance to Toronto on the horizontal axis. What relationship does the graph show?

15. Why should the density of population be higher closer to the central part of the city and be lower towards the edge of the city, as the map and the graph reveal? Why should the density of population be low again in the very heart of the city?

16. What problems might be experienced in providing services (such as electricity, water, sewage, transportation, shopping facilities, and entertainment) to:
    a) areas with very high population densities?
    b) areas with very low population densities?
    Which kind of area would be the most expensive to service?

In discussing the general characteristics of cities you will doubtless have suggested a variety of apparently important characteristics which most cities seem to share. This complexity of urban features – the diversity of jobs, the nature of jobs, the high density of population, and so on – sometimes make it difficult to define urban centres precisely. Can we define an urban centre as a place with a high density of population, in which most people's work does not involve agriculture? The census figures of all countries try to take this kind of question into account, and they illustrate the difficulties involved. For example, in India, to be classified as a town, a settlement has to have more than 5,000 inhabitants, a population density of over 1,000 people per square mile, and 75 per cent of its men engaged in non-agricultural activities. By contrast, the Dominion Bureau of Statistics in Canada defines as "urban" all villages, towns, and cities with populations of over 1,000, together with the fringes of all towns and cities of over 5,000. At the other extreme, in Denmark a settlement only has to have 200 inhabitants to be classified as a town!

17. Why are different definitions for towns required in different countries?
18. What difference would it make to the percentages given in Table 1-1 if Canada were to adopt:
   a) the classification used in India?
   b) the classification used in Denmark?

For the time being, we will define "city" as a relatively large, relatively dense (by Canadian standards) concentration of people where most of the working population are employed in a variety of commercial and industrial activities (rather than in agricultural activities). It is the increase in the numbers of such centres and in their sizes – as most of the people in the nation come to live in them – that is the most basic feature of the phenomenon we call the "urbanization" of Canada.

4. Differences Between and Within Cities

Paradoxically, one of the generalizations we can make about cities is that they are different. Although they are all big, they do vary in size. Although they do have high population densities, these too vary from one city to another, and from one part of the same city to another. Although they all contain a variety of different economic activities, there is not always the same variety in every city, and some cities (in India, for example) actually contain substantial agricultural populations. We do not need to visit many cities to know that they also vary a good deal in their character and to realize that the feelings we have about them may be different. Even within Canada, there is a world of difference between Victoria and St. John's, or between Montreal and Toronto.

Thus, although we know that cities have many characteristics in common, though we have noted the similarities, we do not have to travel far to know that cities may also be different one from another. What are these differences related to? Some of them can be related to the part of the country in which the city is found, for even in a young country like Canada, distinctive styles of architecture and town planning have appeared at different times in different

George Allen Aerial Photos Ltd.

Fig. 1-6 Aerial view of Chemainus, B.C.

places. Others are related to the economic activities which predominate in different urban centres, and others to the cultural characteristics of the urban population and urban immigrants.

Figures 1-6 and 1-7 show aerial views of two small urban centres of approximately similar size. Differences in economic activity are among the most important distinctions between centres and may be discussed first.

19. Using the evidence of the photograph, what are the main economic activities carried on at the urban centre shown in Figure 1-6?
20. In comparison, what are the main activities carried on at the urban centre shown in Figure 1-7?
21. Which economic activities do these two centres share?
22. Which do they not share?

In later parts of this book, we shall be examining in more detail the *functions* of urban centres, or their chief activities and purposes. For example, we can probably guess that the centre shown in Figure 1-6 functions as a centre of the forest products industry and the town shown in Figure 1-7 as a fishing centre. We can pick out buildings which we know are associated with log processing and fishing, and can guess that the majority of the labour force in each town works in these industries.

Fig. 1-7 Aerial view of Lunenburg, N.S.

23. Select the function in column B which best describes each urban centre in column A.

A	B
Ottawa, Ont.	Mining centre
Toronto, Ont.	Port
Kitimat, B.C.	Forest products manufacturing centre
Pine Point, N.W.T.	Administrative centre
Ocean Falls, B.C.	Multi-purpose centre
Sept Îles, Qué.	Mineral processing centre

Not only do urban centres differ among themselves, but important differences in the urban landscape can be found within each city. This is because different parts of the city have developed at different times, and are used for different purposes. Moreover, some parts have only been used for one purpose and have only one *land use* while others have been used for a succession of purposes, a succession of land uses, each of which has probably left its mark. For example, if we look carefully at the busy office district in the centre of a large city, we shall often see evidence of its former residential land use, in the form of a few old rundown private houses squeezed in between tall office buildings.

Fig. 1-8 Land use on the fringes of downtown

24. What succession of land uses has probably been experienced by the area shown in Figure 1-8? What is your evidence?
25. Why might this area have experienced a succession of land uses?
26. Why might the houses in the foreground have fallen into disrepair?

We shall be discussing the differences in land use within the city in more detail in a later section. At this point, we stress only that these different, specialized parts of the city are not separate but, on the contrary, are highly interdependent. It may be helpful to compare towns and cities to machines in that they consist of a complicated arrangement of specialized parts, all of which depend upon each other to some extent. Residential subdivisions would not be built unless jobs were available in industrial or business areas of the city. Shopping centres could not exist without the customers from nearby residential subdivisions. And so on. The couplings of the machine, the links between parts of the city, are the communications networks – roads, subways, streetcar lines, telephones – which enable us, as city dwellers, to move from one specialized part of the city to another and to participate fully in the city's life.

5. A Word About Viewpoints

A geographical viewpoint can provide a useful starting point from which to tackle the complex problems of the modern city. The geographical viewpoint stresses the *location* of things – why people do what they do where they do it – and this often lies at the root of many an urban problem. Geography also provides a means of investigating the patterns we see in an urban landscape, and can lead us to identify the social processes that underlie the formation of these landscapes. Interest in cities, however, is shared by disciplines such as history, economics, sociology, planning, and anthropology. Indeed, so great do the problems of the modern city seem that practically every subject among the social sciences, and many among the physical and applied sciences, contains at least one branch which is devoted to urban study. Though the geographical viewpoint is used here as a basis for study, it is supplemented as widely as possible by the insights and methods of enquiry of other subjects.

This book contains a mixture of things for you to read and things for you to do, projects which suggest how interesting the city can be. The graphs, tables, photographs, maps, and documentary excerpts which appear in the following pages are only samples of the sorts of evidence which you can gather to increase your understanding of the city. You will certainly be able to gather useful data from a great number of sources, and better yet, to observe the urban environment at first hand by walking around the streets with an observing eye and an enquiring mind.

As students, we are led to look at things in a particular way and to ask questions about them by the work of others. Ideas about the city, like ideas about anything else, are the result of the work of many scholars. Many people have contributed towards the concept of the city which we shall examine together in this book, and their contribution must be acknowledged. At the end of the book you will see a selection of readings which you may find interesting and which can assist you in further study of those ideas. So read on, and enjoy your exploration of the urban environment!

TWO

The Growth of Canadian Cities

1.   Introduction

Every city has a history which is reflected in its buildings, its streets, and the attitudes of its people. Though our cities are new compared with many of those of the Old World, they are old enough to have developed distinctive characteristics. To a large extent, different characteristics result from cities having grown up at different times and under different economic conditions and cultural influences; their central cores contain different street patterns, businesses, and architectural styles. Canada's urban geography is of recent origin, but it is more recent in some parts of the country than in others. Thus the historical scale is different for each city, so that "Old Quebec" dates from the seventeenth century and "Old Vancouver" from the nineteenth. Since the conditions for urban growth have been different in each historical period the ways in which cities have expanded have also varied. Some, at least, of the suburban growth of Quebec, Montreal, and Toronto took place in the horse and buggy era, while Vancouver's early growth occurred rapidly along electric streetcar lines.

Fortunately for us, cities are not pulled down and built afresh in each succeeding generation, though the pace of office and apartment construction might sometimes suggest that they are. Instead, they evolve in a way which always leaves something of the past behind, even if only in the shape of a small private house dwarfed by surrounding office buildings or in the direction taken by a street. Indeed, because they belong to the public rather than to private individuals, streets are among the most durable of urban features so that often twentieth-century traffic moves with difficulty over a nineteenth-century street pattern. By learning how to "read" the streets and other evidence of the ways in which cities have grown, we can discover a great deal about our urban environment and, in doing so, value the past that has shaped it.

In this section we shall look at five characteristic types of city which have appeared at different times in Canada's past. Our examination will in no sense try to represent the entire course of Canadian urban history, but rather it will try to look in detail at selected cases which seem to exemplify certain important trends. Colonial New France was preoccupied with defence and its towns and cities, of which Quebec was the most important, were defensive centres above all. In later and safer times, they formed the cores of great ports like Montreal, which grew through the trade in staple products which characterized this period

in Canadian history. The westward spread of the railways spawned a new breed
of city of which Winnipeg is an example, while at the same time industrialization came to Hamilton and the urban centres of the east.

The story of Canada is, from one point of view, that of an outward shift of
a frontier from the original settled areas of the Atlantic Coast, the St. Lawrence
lowlands, the Red River Valley and the southern Pacific Coast. Thus it is appropriate that our last example should be the frontier town of Thompson, for it
represents a modern example of a consistent theme in Canadian history: many
Canadian cities have been frontier towns at some time. Similarly, many Canadian cities have been fortresses, ports, and railway and industrial centres in
the past. Consequently we should expect to find many of the features we shall
examine in Quebec, Montreal, Winnipeg, and Hamilton in many other urban
centres including, perhaps, our own.

2.   The Fortress City

Though many of Canada's first settlers were farmers, the land was not con-
quered entirely from the farm, but from the urban centres on which the farm
depended for protection. Control of the land was exercised from fortress towns
like Louisburg, Quebec and Montreal which provided security from the invader
for seigneur and tenant alike, and which also gave them some access to the
outside world. Quebec is certainly the closest we can come in North America
to the cities of mediaeval Europe, for it was built as part of a mediaeval system.
Behind its protecting walls, now unique in a North American city, Canada's
first urban people lived in a way which was not too dissimilar to that lived by
their contemporaries across the Atlantic.

THE QUEBEC OF SAMUEL DE CHAMPLAIN (1608)

Quebec City was almost certainly the first urban centre in Canada and like the
later French fortress towns of Montreal and Louisburg, it was established to
provide protection for an agricultural colony and to maintain a foothold in
North America for France. Though it is very likely that Jacques Cartier had
set up a small settlement close to the present location of Quebec City in 1535,
the city owes its origin more to the explorer Samuel de Champlain, who erected
a *habitation* there in 1608. His journal describes his first impressions of the
place and the first attempts at building a settlement.

> From the Island of Orleans to Quebec the distance is a league. I
> arrived there on the 3rd of July, when I searched for a place suit-
> able for our settlement, but I could find none more convenient or
> better situated than the point of Quebec, so called by the savages,
> which was covered with nut-trees. I at once employed a portion
> of our workmen in cutting them down, that we might construct
> our habitation there: one I set to sawing boards, another to mak-
> ing a cellar and digging ditches, another I sent to Tadoussac with

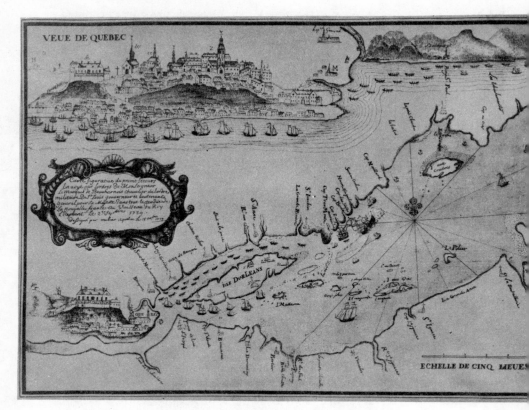

Fig. 2-1 Map of the St. Lawrence River, showing the location of Quebec, 1729

the barque to get supplies. The first thing we made was the store-house for keeping under cover our supplies, which was promptly accomplished through the zeal of all, and my attention to the work.

W. L. Grant, ed., *Voyages of Samuel de Champlain, 1604-1618* (New York: Barnes and Noble, 1907), pp. 131-2.

I had the work on our quarters continued, which was composed of three buildings of two stories. Each one was three fathoms long, and two and a half wide. The storehouse was six fathoms long and three wide, with a fine cellar six feet deep. I had a gallery made all around our buildings, on the outside, at the second story, which proved very convenient. There were also ditches, fifteen feet wide and six deep. On the outer side of the ditches, I constructed several spurs, which enclosed a part of the dwelling, at the points where we placed our cannon. Before the habitation there is a place four fathoms wide and six or seven long, looking out upon the river-bank. Surrounding the habitation are very good gardens, and a place on the north side some hundred or

Lockwood Survey Corp. Ltd.

Fig. 2-2 Quebec today

hundred and twenty paces long and fifty or sixty wide. Moreover, near Quebec, there is a little river, coming from a lake in the interior, distant six or seven leagues from our settlement.

Ibid., pp. 136-7.

1. Had you been Champlain what characteristics would you have looked for in the site of your *habitation?*
2. From the evidence of Figures 2-1 and 2-2, did the site chosen have these characteristics?
3. From the documentary evidence of Champlain's journal, what did he do to enhance the natural characteristics of the site?
4. Which of the site's characteristics were important in 1608 and 1729 but not now? Which are important now but were not then?

In the questions above we have used the word "site" several times. The site of any urban centre is of great importance since it must satisfy a number of essential needs. Some of these needs are shared by all urban centres; for example, there are very few whose sites do not provide an adequate supply of drinking water. Other needs are related to the urban centre's specific function (page 10). Champlain's *habitation* would have required access to drinking water, agricultural land, and safe anchorage whatever its proposed functions had been, but since it was to be a fortress the existence of a high promontory overlooking the river was evidently an advantage.

Other urban centres have site requirements different from those of Quebec. Many towns have grown up at *bridging points* where the narrowing of a river permits a bridge to be built and therefore attracts routes from both sides. *Gap points* provide analogous sites, where routes converge to pass through a gap in a line of hills or mountains. Other towns have grown up where the physical conditions require goods to be transferred from one mode of transportation to another as, for example, at the head of navigation of a river or system of lakes. Such towns are said to occupy *break-of-bulk points*. Perhaps the most obvious site requirement of all is that of ports which, of course, have need of a suitable *harbour*.

This is not to say that man is not often called upon to adapt a site to his needs if the characteristics which Nature has provided are unsuitable. Many of the world's great ports now have harbours which are artificial or have been modified by human effort. The Port of Vancouver occupies the natural harbour of Burrard Inlet, but the neighbouring Roberts Bank Superport is entirely artificial. By the same token, the site requirements which have led to a town's establishment often become redundant, sometimes even inhibiting a town's future growth. In Quebec, as political circumstances changed, the original site factors lost their importance, and the city expanded into the flat areas of the St. Charles River which had been ignored as long as defence was an important consideration. A town may continue to grow and prosper long after its original site characteristics have ceased to be of any importance.

---

5. Make a list of the site requirements which are shared by all urban centres.
6. What additional site requirements, if any, are the following likely to have: a route centre, a mining town, a port, a capital city?
7. What site characteristics might have favoured the establishment of Toronto, Ottawa, Calgary, Edmonton, Halifax, and Vancouver?
8. Match the following urban centres with the type of site they occupy.

Thunder Bay, Ont.	Gap point
Edmonton	Harbour
Halifax	Break-of-bulk point
Fernie, B.C.	Bridge point
Lunenburg, N.S.	Break-of-bulk point and harbour

9. What site factors might have been considered in the establishment of your own town? Which additional site factors have encouraged and which have inhibited its growth?

---

3.   The Port City

As settlement increased, fortresses became less important than ports. The development of Canada has to a large extent depended upon such staple products as fish, furs, and forest products, all of which require an overseas market. Ports

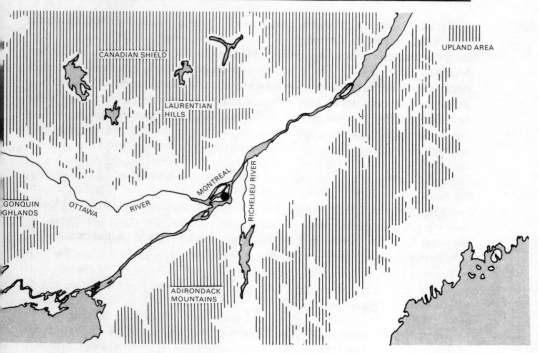

Fig. 2-3 The situation of Montreal

have therefore been the focus of a very important sector of our economic life for most of our history. Even at the present time, a longshoremen's or grain handlers' strike can have more repercussions throughout the country than a strike by almost any other group. In the past, flourishing ports like Montreal, Quebec, and Halifax have thronged with merchants whose activities have in large measure directed the country's growth.

Like the fortress city, a port has certain site requirements. A sheltered harbour is an advantage. More important still, the general *situation* must be such as to give ready access to inland areas whose trade the port will be able to tap. As pointed out earlier, though a port may often exist without favourable site characteristics, it rarely does so without an advantageous situation.

The location of Montreal illustrates the concepts of both site and situation. It was sited at the natural head of navigation of the St. Lawrence River and, like Quebec, at a point which could be fortified easily. Both characteristics are important, but had Montreal not possessed corresponding advantages of situation it is doubtful if it could have become the great port that it is today.

The situational advantages of a city are often associated with its surrounding topography. Note in Figure 2-3 how the upstanding areas of the Laurentian, Adirondack, and Algonquin highlands funnel routeways to the Montreal lowland, while the Richelieu valley provides access to the south. The Ottawa Valley route between the Laurentian and Algonquin uplands was particularly important in Montreal's early days and helped the Montreal merchants to gain control over much of the fur trade of the interior by providing them with relatively easy access to the fur supplying areas.

In later times, the natural routes were followed when building railways, since these routes had few steep (and therefore costly) grades. The St. Lawrence and Atlantic Railway joined Montreal to Portland, Maine, via the Richelieu valley in 1853, thus freeing it to a certain extent from its icebound winter condition: and the CPR struck out for the west along the Ottawa Valley in 1871. Situational advantages given by nature are thus often strengthened by the building of lines of communications along these natural corridors.

THE PORT OF MONTREAL (1816 and 1870)

Following its selection as a possible settlement by Champlain in 1611, Montreal grew from a tiny fortified trading post to a port of international significance. In its early days it traded in the staples of the country, especially furs. With the opening of the Canadian West and the introduction of the steamship, its trade increased both in volume and diversity. In the latter part of the nineteenth century it was connected to Europe by regular steam packet service.

The Montreal *Herald,* June 29, 1816

The Harbor of Montreal now contains about thirty square-rigged vessels, which mostly came with pretty full cargoes. The number of craft is also very considerable. Although such a number of vessels indicates a great and active commerce, yet this is not the case; business is remarkably dull and scarcely an article meets a ready market, at good prices. – Except Pot and Pearl Ashes, and Lumber, we have no produce this season to make returns, and even these will go but a wretchedly short length to pay for such enormous imports as we have this year. We are not sure if the exports (furs excepted) will much more than pay for the Provisions imported from Britain and Ireland. What, also, renders the prospect very uncheering, is the probability of bills of exchange being at a considerable premium; that is, much greater than it is now.

Laurence M. Wilson, *This was Montreal* (Montreal: Chateau de Ramezay, 1960), p. 111.

---

10. What significant change had occurred between 1816 and 1853 in the type of ship entering the Port of Montreal? (Refer to Table 2-1.)
11. What commodity prevented the balance of trade with Great Britain from being unfavourable in 1815?
12. Draw a graph showing the tonnage of shipping entering the Port of Montreal between 1853 and 1869. How might you account for the change?
13. Find out what changes had taken place in Montreal's transportation links with the rest of the country between 1816 and 1870.

A port's situation is usually such as to provide it with relatively easy access to the area lying behind it, the trade of which it controls. The area is called the port's *hinterland,* which means literally "the land behind." Though access to

Table 2-1   Volume of Traffic in the Port of Montreal

Years	Different Steamers	Trips	Tonnage	First Arrival in Port
1853	3	4	1,951	May 10th
1854	4	5	4,052	June 2nd
1855				
1856	6	15	15,701	May 9th
1857	7	6	5,275	
1858	6	16	19,064	May 5th
1859	8	35	43,886	May 3rd
1860	12	36	44,298	May 2nd
1861	13	38	51,033	
1862	15	51	61,177	May 1st
1863	15	46	54,356	May 9th
1864	14	43	55,480	May 6th
1865	16	60	75,463	May 3rd
1866	21	59	69,595	May 3rd
1867	25	82	77,622	May 4th
1868	23	93	96,887	May 4th
1869	24			April 30th

SOURCE: Alfred Sandham, *Montreal, Past and Present* (Montreal: George Bishop & Co., 1870), p. 216.

the hinterland may be favoured by the existence of natural routes, the port's growth depends upon transportation lines linking the port and its hinterland. As stated railways, canals, and roads can reinforce the advantages conferred by a good natural situation. Montreal's growth depended upon the building of railway links first with Upper Canada in 1856 *via* the Grand Trunk Railway and with the Pacific coast *via* the Canadian Pacific Railway, and upon the improvement of the St. Lawrence waterway. The growth in both extent and productivity of the hinterland is clearly reflected in the growth of the port city itself as is shown by Figures 2-4, and 2-5.

14. The walls of the city as shown in the map of 1761 (Figure 2-4) are outlined in the aerial photograph. Trace the streets which existed in 1761. How do you account for the fact that the street pattern remained while buildings changed? What problems might this bring about at the present time?
15. What differences can be observed between the street pattern of 1761, and that which was added afterwards?
16. What changes occurred in the port and transportation facilities of Montreal between 1761 and the present?
17. How might these be related to the changes which had taken place in Montreal's trade and in its growing links with the rest of the country?
18. Compare Figures 2-5 and 3-3. Locate the area of the Old Town in Figure 3-3.
19. What are the relative advantages of studying cities by using maps (as in Figure 2-4), vertical aerial photographs (as in Figure 2-5), or oblique aerial photographs (as in Figure 3-3)?

Fig. 2-4 Map of Montreal by Jean Rocque, 1761

Fig. 2-5 Aerial view of Montreal

4.   The Railway City

The building of the railways favoured not only the growth of ports but of inland cities across Canada. It has sometimes been said that Canada is a "geographical impossibility tied together with railways." Certainly in a very real sense the majority of Canadian cities owe their growth and present dimensions to the railway. It is sometimes difficult to imagine a Canada apart from the railways which brought it political and economic unity. In particular, the shape of urban Canada was controlled by the westward spread of the rail network, when hitherto insignificant trading posts sprang into life as modern cities as they were touched by the "end of steel."

WINNIPEG AND THE COMING OF THE RAILWAY (1872 and 1881)

Perhaps Winnipeg exemplifies the railway era better than any other city. Fort Garry had been both a trading post and centre for the tiny Red River Settlement. The first train reached St. Boniface in 1878 and two years later a bridge was constructed across the Red River. The village had become a city. As immigrants poured into the opening agricultural lands of the prairies and their productivity burgeoned, Winnipeg assumed the role of both principal point of entry for homesteaders and the natural collection point for their first harvests.

The Immigrant Sheds

Are situated to the east of Fort Garry, near the mouth of the Assiniboine or at its confluence with the Red River. These buildings comprise two separate ranges, capable of accommodating four or five hundred persons, and provided with many conveniences. They are the best of all the immigrant sheds that we have seen between Thunder Bay and Winnipeg. The immigrant generally makes this his home until he selects a location.

Something About Lots

The following scale of prices will show the advance of real estate within the city:

Average price per Lot	In 1871	In 1874
H. B. Co's Estate (Main Street)	$1,000	$2,000
McDermot Estate	75	300
Morris Estate	50	200
Magnus Brown Estate	10	50
Schultz Estate	50	300

Real estate, although appearing high to the resident of an eastern city, is still very low when the prospects of the city are taken into consideration. There are already three railroads projected from it, two lines of navigation to the Rocky Mountains already exist-

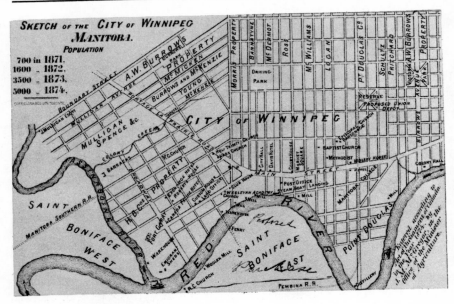

Fig. 2-6 Winnipeg in 1874

ing, making their junction here, and with a trade and commerce which rank it already the sixth city in the Dominion.

Speculation may be said not to have been inaugurated yet, though one operator, Mr. Burrows, has sold over 400 city lots during the past year.

This gentleman has done very much towards making the city known by his extensive advertising; and he has displayed unusual enterprise in attracting investments. Having a large tract of some 200 acres – the Magnus Brown property – he has not only laid it out and planned it with a fine park in the centre, but dug a drain of two miles in length, and laid down a sidewalk for nearly a mile, and finished up by giving away fifty lots free, to attract residents, which wise and liberal course has repaid him a hundredfold, and a number of residences now dot the prairie, where a year ago, the long grass waved; and the growth of the city is now permanently fixed in that direction.

George Elliot, *Winnipeg As It Is In 1874* (Winnipeg: Daily Free Press 1874), pp. 15 and 25-26.

1881 – Winnipeg is London or New York on a small scale. You meet people from almost every part of the world. Ask a man on the street for direction, and the chances are ten to one that he answers, "I have just arrived sir." Friends meet who parted last on the other side of the globe, and with a hasty "What! you here too?", each passes on his way, probably to a real-estate office or auction room. The writer saw Winnipeg first in 1872. It consisted of a few rickety-looking shanties that looked as if they had been dropped promiscuously on the verge of a boundless prairie. The poorest inhabitant seemed willing to give any one a lot or an acre. And now, land on Main Street and the streets adjoining is held at higher figures than in the centre of Toronto; and Winnipeggers, in referring to the future, never make comparisons with any city smaller than Chicago.

Principal Grant of Queen's University quoted in W. J. Healy, *Winnipeg's Early Days* (Winnipeg: Stovel Co. Ltd., 1927), p. 21.

20. What purpose did immigrant sheds serve in Winnipeg? Find their location in Figure 2-6.
21. What is the meaning of the term "speculation" as used in the first reading? What evidence is there that land speculation was very active in the 1870's. Why should this have been so?
22. Why would land speculation have been favoured by a grid pattern of streets and lots as shown in Figure 2-6? Why would the rectangular grid be broken by such streets as Portage la Prairie Road (the present-day Portage Avenue) and by Main Street?
23. What kinds of industry and service might have been found in Winnipeg at this time?

By the end of the nineteenth century, Winnipeg had become a railway city completely. Not only were railways routed through the city (as shown in Figure 2-7) favouring its role as a distribution centre, but industries which were associated both with this role and with the railways themselves developed greatly. Where goods of any kind converge, storage and sometime primary manufacturing facilities spring up. Thus, by 1900 Winnipeg was already a centre for grain elevators, flour mills, stockyards, and meat packing plants. It had become the major *entrepôt,* or storage and distribution point for the whole of western Canada.

24. What evidence is there from Figure 2-7 that Winnipeg was a major communications centre in 1882? What types of transport might have been used on mail routes which did not follow railway lines?
25. Find the destination of the railway lines shown in Figure 2-7. What was the probable extent of the area served by Winnipeg at this time?
26. Refer to an historical atlas to find out in what order the railways were built. How might this have affected Winnipeg's growth?
27. What features of the natural topography favoured Winnipeg's situation?
28. What evidence is there in Figure 2-8 that industry might be associated with railways?
29. What effect, if any, has a railway had upon the growth of the town or city in which you live?
30. What problems might railway centres like Winnipeg experience today, both with regard to their internal forms and their economies?

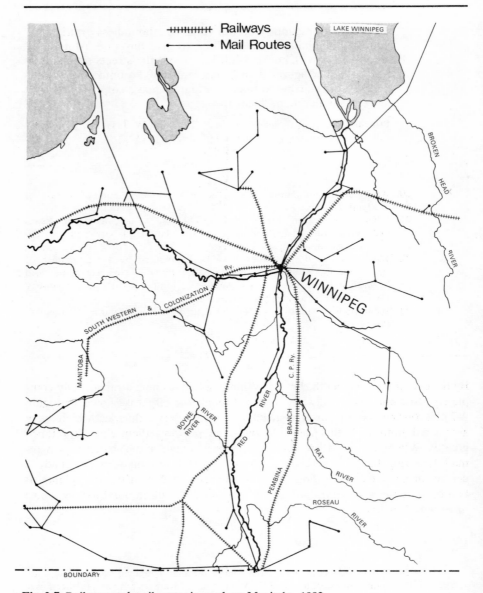

Fig. 2-7 Railways and mail routes in southern Manitoba, 1882

5.   The Industrial City

Generally speaking, industrialization came later to Canadian cities than to American cities and was not on as large a scale. Until the Second World War spurred the growth of secondary industries, the bulk of the country's labour force was employed in activities other than manufacturing. Some Canadian

Fig. 2-8 CPR railway yards in Winnipeg today

cities did develop manufacturing industries fairly early, but often in association with parallel developments in the United States. While the Western Provinces remained concerned with the primary industries of forestry, mining, and agriculture, manufacturing began to develop in southern Ontario to process local agricultural products or as an offshoot of the manufacturing belt of the northeastern United States.

Industrial growth in North America, as in Western Europe, had a number of undesirable consequences. The factories which were built in the towns attracted vast numbers of migrants – from the countryside in the case of Western Europe, and from overseas in the case of North America. Often the urban factory workers were employed for very long hours under appalling conditions, a fact which was to lead to the growth of socialist movements, trade unions, and eventually to reform. They were housed in cheaply-built and crowded accommodation which was seldom more than a few hundred yards from the factory since people invariably walked to work until the streetcar provided them with a greater choice as to where they might live.

The result in the cities of both Western Europe and North America was probably the most depressing urban landscape that has ever been created. Workers' houses were pushed together into rows so that land yielded as much rent as possible, and services were either inadequate or non-existent. And over all hung the customary pall of yellow smoke which generally hid the sun. This was the era in which the majority of urban *slums* were built, slums which exist even today in many cities despite extensive schemes of urban renewal. It was the age also when cities emerged basically in the form in which we now know them, with civic buildings, railway depots, department stores, streetcars and bus lines, schools and universities, and factories.

INDUSTRIAL HAMILTON (1852 and 1913)

Of all Canadian cities, Hamilton perhaps best expresses the kind of growth that was taking place in the industrial cities of Western Europe and the United States. From a market town of 14,000 people in 1851 it became an industrial centre with a population of 100,000 and over 400 industries sixty years later. Like the cities of the American manufacturing belt, Hamilton's increase in population was largely made up of immigrants from Europe, especially from Ireland. Also, like Pittsburgh, Cleveland, Toledo, and Gary, its economic growth was based on the steel industry. It differed from these centres only in that its industrialization was later in starting and on a smaller scale . . . .

Consider three men who lived in Hamilton, Ontario, in the early 1850's.

E. McGarry, a thirty-year-old Roman Catholic laborer born in Ireland lived in a two-story frame house on Merrick Street, which he rented for £ 11 a year. With him lived his wife, two sons aged seven and five, and his two-year-old daughter. Sharing the house were McGarry's twenty-five-year-old laborer brother, his young wife and infant daughter. Aside from his rent, McGarry reported £ 3 of personal property and his earnings averaged less than £ 1 a week. Although he must have lived always on the edge of economic disaster, McGarry was a bit more well-off than three-quarters of the laborers in Hamilton.

J. McFatradge, a forty-year-old Presbyterian shoemaker also born in Ireland, owned his own house, a two-storey frame dwelling on Vine Street assessed at £ 9 annual value; his income was £ 50 per year. McFatradge's family consisted of his thirty-five-year-old wife, also born in Ireland and his five children, two sons aged twelve and six and three daughters aged fifteen, four, and two; the McFatradges kept one boarder but no servants.

J. D. Pringle, prosperous young Canadian-born lawyer and member of the Church of Scotland, rented a house on Merrick Street for which he paid the enormous sum of £ 45; he earned a solid £ 150 per year. Pringle, aged thirty-two, had a twenty-three-year-old wife and a two-year-old daughter. Naturally enough, the well-off Pringles kept a servant.

Messrs. McGarry, McFatradge, and Pringle did nothing in particular that justifies their rescue from historical oblivion. They were perfectly ordinary and unremarkable citizens of a mid-

nineteenth century city. Yet their very lack of historical importance gives them a significance from one point of view, for these
were, in fact, men "representative" of the Hamilton population
in certain ways.

Michael B. Katz, "Social Structure in Hamilton, Ontario," in Stephen
Thernstrom and Richard Sennett, eds., *Nineteenth Century Cities* (New
Haven: Yale University Press, 1969), pp. 209-214.

INTERNATIONAL HARVESTER COMPANY OF CANADA, LIMITED

Chicago, Ill.
1913

Commissioner of Industries,
Hamilton, Ontario.
Dear Sir.

We take pleasure in answering your inquiry as to why the
Deering Harvester Company originally located at Hamilton, and
why this Company has, since 1902, continued to develop the
plant that was acquired from the Deering Harvester Company.
A careful survey of all the principal Canadian towns and cities
was made to find the point that offered the most advantages for
the manufacture of agricultural implements, and the City of
Hamilton was selected for many reasons, chief among which are
the following:

1. From a shipping standpoint this location was very attractive because the Company was able to purchase land on
   the Bay and maintain its own docks, thus affording a harbor
   on the Great Lakes.
2. The railroad facilities afforded connections to five different
   roads, and the combination of these facilities in close
   proximity to the water front makes possible rail and water
   shipments.
3. The location of Hamilton geographically makes an almost
   ideal place from which to ship agricultural implements to
   the great wheat raising country of Western Canada, as well
   as to the seaboard for export trade.
4. An important factor is the electric power that can be pro-
   cured on a reasonable basis from the Hamilton Electric
   Light and Cataract Power Company.
5. For an industry like ours Hamilton is a most satisfactory
   location because of its low rents, and its close proximity to
   the great fruit and vegetable farms.

We feel sure that any new industry locating in Hamilton may
expect to receive the same fair and just treatment from you that

has always been accorded our Company, and we therefore, believe that it is a most desirable and advantageous site for the location of a manufacturing plant.

Very truly yours,
Cyrus H. McCormick

City Council, *Hamilton, Canada* (Hamilton: Lister & Co., 1913), p. 95.

Table 2-2   **Hamilton Industrial Growth, 1911-13**

HAMILTON	1911-12	1912-13
Population	81,000	100,000
Industries	375	415
No. of Employees	22,000	27,000
Capital Invested	$40,000,000	$50,000,000
Wages Paid	$13,000,000	$15,000,000
Yearly Value of Output	$40,000,000	$60,000,000
Average Wage Rate per capita in Hamilton	**$556**	
Average Wage Rate per capita throughout Canada	**$475**	
Investment of American capital in plants during last 10 years	$25,000,000	

SOURCE: City Council, *Hamilton, Canada*, p. 200.

31. What do the brief biographical sketches given in the first reading suggest about the occupational and social structure of Hamilton before industrialization? What changes would you expect to be brought about by the coming of industry?
32. In the letter of testimonial sent to the Commissioner of Industries in 1913, reasons are given for locating the International Harvester Company in Hamilton. Which of these refer to advantages of site and which to advantages of situation?
33. What other types of industry would you expect to have located in Hamilton in order to take advantage of the same factors?
34. Figure 2-9 shows a map of Hamilton before the greater part of its industrial growth had taken place. Where would you expect industries to locate in order to best exploit the site advantages mentioned in the second reading?
35. To what extent do Table 2-3 and Figure 2-10 confirm the expectations suggested by your answers to Questions 31 and 34?
36. The data in Table 2-2 suggest that certain changes occurred in Hamilton between 1911 and 1913. What would these changes be? What is the significance of the last item on the table?
37. Examine the major industries of your own town or city. What factors may have led to their being located in your town?

Industrialization came to Hamilton with the railways and expanded as American companies grew larger and looked for investment opportunities abroad. Thus the story of Hamilton's industrialization is parallel to that of many other Can-

Table 2-3   Occupations and wages in Hamilton, 1961

	Percentage	Average Annual Income	
		Men	Women
All occupations	100		
White-collar workers	40		
Managerial	8	$7,336	$3,712
Professional and Technical	10	$5,875	$3,309
Clerical	14	$3,747	$2,338
Sales	8	$4,241	$1,304
Blue-collar workers	39		
Craftsmen, production process	33	$4,274	$2,068
Labourers	6	$2,698	$1,645
Transport and communications	6	$3,647	$2,174
Service and recreation	11	$3,036	$1,242
Primary occupations	3	—	—
Occupation not stated	1	—	—

SOURCE: Dominion Bureau of Statistics, *Census of Canada* (Ottawa: Queen's Printer, 1961).

Fig. 2-9 Hamilton, Ont., in 1875

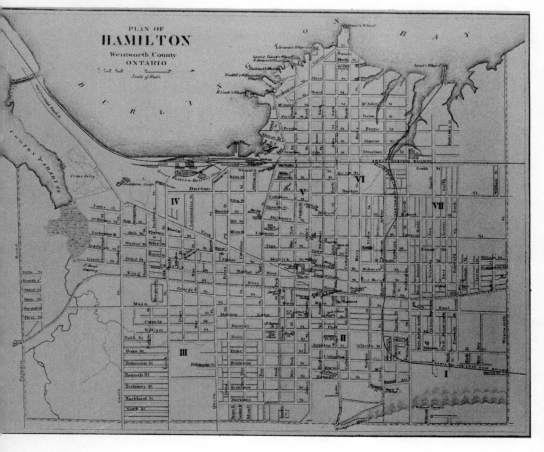

adian cities. By 1855, Hamilton had become an important rail centre and was linked by the Great Western Railway to Niagara Falls and the United States rail network in one direction, and to Toronto and the Grand Trunk Railway in the other. Its first major industry was a rolling mill erected in 1864 to provide rails for the Great Western, and this set the course for the future development of its industry. At the turn of the century, large American companies like International Harvester, and Canadian companies like the Steel Company of Canada Limited (Stelco) also located here and Hamilton's position as the major steel centre of the country was confirmed.

Fig. 2-10 Aerial view of Hamilton waterfront

6.   The Frontier City

Most of Canada's urban centres are to be found in the southern part of the country, less than 200 miles from the United States border. They form a long narrow belt across the country. Although many centres were isolated to begin with, they were eventually overtaken by the agricultural frontier. In the north, however, commercial agriculture is impossible at present, and whatever urban development has taken place there rests on quite different foundations. Both the Western Cordillera and the Canadian Shield have abundant forest, mineral, and energy resources which have provided the basis for economic growth. Because these resources are often found far from populated areas, however, completely new towns have to be created to accommodate the labour force required to develop them. Thus, some of Canada's most recent urban growth has occurred not on an agricultural but on a resource frontier.

The towns of the resource frontier are characterized by being remote from the major settled areas of the south, sometimes with no means of transportation except aircraft. To be sure, most are connected to the south by road or railway, but long distances discourage frequent travel and add to the costs of transportation. Consequently, the towns of the resource frontier are often more self-sufficient than towns of similar size in more developed areas both in their economic and social lives. Many of them are *company towns* and are managed by the company which owns the mine or forest operation on which they are based. Increasingly, though, they tend to be developed by the company in co-operation with a provincial authority.

Such a town is Thompson, Manitoba, which was established in 1957 jointly by the Manitoba Provincial Government and the International Nickel Company of Canada Limited (Inco). The reason for its establishment was the discovery the previous year of a major ore body on the Canadian Shield some 400 miles north of Winnipeg. Inco's decision to develop the ore body rested on a number of factors. For example, it lay quite close to the CNR line from The Pas to Churchill, presenting the possibility of good connections with world markets *via* an ocean port. Also, the existence of a potential power site on the nearby Nelson River (later developed as the Kelsey generating station) was an added inducement. The townsite itself was developed to house the families of the men who would work in the Inco plant.

38. Locate the Inco plant in Figures 2-11 and 2-12. Why has the townsite been located some distance away?
39. What evidence can you see from Figure 2-11 that Thompson is a planned settlement?
40. What evidence can you see from Figure 2-12 that further growth is expected there?
41. In what ways do the map and photograph suggest that Thompson is a fairly self-contained settlement? What connections are provided with the outside world?

Fig. 2-11 Aerial view of Thompson, Man.

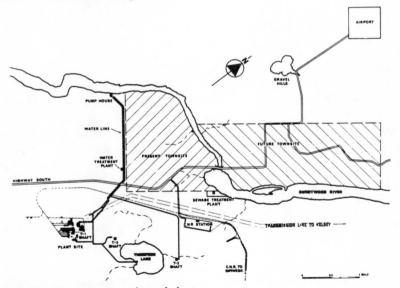

Fig. 2-12 The Thompson townsite and plant

42. Compare Figure 2-11 with Figure 7-3 on p. 122, which shows a new suburban development on the edge of Toronto. What significance is there in the fact that they are similar in some respects?
43. If you were going to live and work in Thompson, what features do you think you would find attractive? What features would you find unattractive?

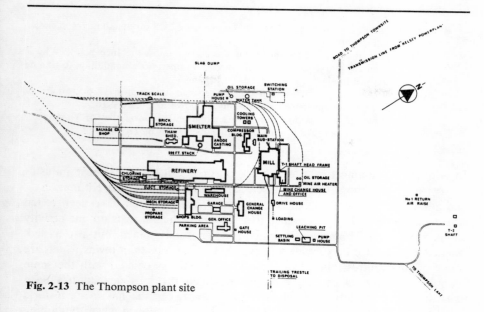

Fig. 2-13 The Thompson plant site

Canada's early mining towns were often little more than camps. At least in the initial stages of development, no attempt was made to provide facilities for families and so they were often almost exclusively male establishments. Dawson City in the 1890's and Yellowknife in the 1930's were settlements of this kind, and though not nearly as rough and tough as they might be portrayed in legend, they certainly lacked many of the amenities which would attract families. Today large industrial companies recognize the importance of drawing wives and children to the towns of the frontier in creating a stable population. Consequently, the majority of homes to be seen in Figure 2-11 are single-family residences arranged in a pattern which consciously attempts to reproduce a suburban development to the south. Even so, a rapid turnover in population is one of the problems with which frontier towns have to cope.

Some stability might be provided to the towns on the frontier if they were to have a greater variety of employment, so that people of different social and economic levels might be attracted to them. The frontier towns are often centres of *primary industry* alone and can provide only a few kinds of jobs, many of them unskilled. Few of these towns develop many *secondary industries* such as processing or fabricating. Occasionally, some processing of raw materials is carried on in the remote towns on the frontier; since transportation costs are so high, it is usually more economical to process raw materials and thus reduce their bulk before shipment. A pulp mill or a metal smelter are examples of secondary industry which fulfill these requirements; a hundred dollars worth of newsprint or metal ingots is less bulky, and therefore cheaper to transport, than a hundred dollars worth of logs or metal ore. However, industries involved in the final stages of processing and fabricating usually prefer to locate in the large towns of the south where their labour costs are lower, where supplies of industry and business services are close at hand, and where the costs of distributing their products to the consumer markets are less.

44. Locate the major buildings shown in Figure 2-13 on the photograph shown in Figure 2-11.
45. How many separate operations are carried on at the Inco plant? Why is it an advantage to have certain secondary operations in addition to mining at the minesite?
46. What are the major differences between the industrial operations of Thompson and those of Hamilton as shown in Figure 2-10?
47. What advantages does Hamilton's situation have over that of Thompson?
48. What factors favour both the site and situation of Thompson?

In addition to mining towns, Canada's north is dotted with forest industry centres like Marathon, Ont., hydroelectric power centres like Kitimat, B.C., and administrative centres like Inuvik, N.W.T. All are what have been called *single-enterprise communities* since their economic health rests on one activity alone. Towns like Thompson, in which ore is not only mined, but also milled, smelted, and refined do provide a greater variety of jobs than towns which are solely mining centres, but all of these jobs are still associated with the same economic activity. Once the resource on which the jobs depend has been exhausted then the jobs themselves cease to exist. Canada has many historic *ghost towns* like Barkerville, B.C., that have been abandoned when the mining activity which brought them to life came to an end.

Some such towns have been able to find alternative economic activities. For example, although Yellowknife's gold mines will not continue to produce forever, the town is now assured stability as the capital of the Northwest Territories. This question of economic stability is discussed further in Part Three. Here we can note that many towns on the frontier will probably find it impossible to diversify their activities to any extent in future, and can have no destiny other than to become ghost towns. The solution of the *non-permanent planned community* has been suggested for this problem. Such a community would consist of pre-fabricated buildings, to be dismantled and easily moved when no longer required at a location where, say, a mineral resource had been exhausted. The closest examples we have at present of this kind of community are the oil camps of the far north, but these are not really urban centres at all. Until such communities are feasible, generally only the largest and most promising ore bodies will be developed, since it is not worth putting a large investment into a townsite whose expected life will only be a matter of a few years.

49. Which economic activities shown in Figure 2-14 have given rise to the greatest number of new settlements?
50. The majority of the more remote towns have been established after 1940. Why should this be so?
51. Compare Figure 2-14 with an atlas map. Which of the new towns are connected to the south by road or rail?
52. Why are most of the new towns on the Canadian Shield?

Sometimes it is assumed that the northern frontier will be filled up as was the frontier in the south, even though our present technology cannot support productive agriculture in the far north. It is sometimes argued that a closely knit network

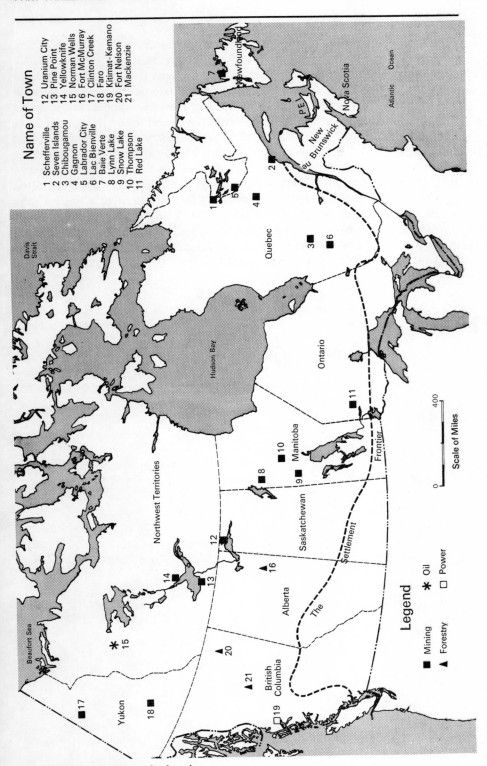

Name of Town

1 Schefferville
2 Seven Islands
3 Chibougamou
4 Gagnon
5 Labrador City
6 Lac Bienville
7 Baie Verte
8 Lynn Lake
9 Snow Lake
10 Thompson
11 Red Lake
12 Uranium City
13 Pine Point
14 Yellowknife
15 Norman Wells
16 Fort McMurray
17 Clinton Creek
18 Faro
19 Kitimat-Kemano
20 Fort Nelson
21 Mackenzie

Legend

■ Mining
▲ Forestry
* Oil
□ Power

Scale of Miles
0 400

Fig. 2-14 New towns on the frontier

of cities and towns need not rest only on an agricultural base. In Siberia, where conditions are very similar to those of the Canadian North, towns like Norilsk with a population of 130,000 have been built far from the agricultural areas to the south. We might ask whether this degree of urban development is possible in the Canadian North – or indeed desirable? Recently, some have suggested that thought be given to the development of towns and transportation facilities in the middle North, the so-called *Mid-Canada Corridor*. Those who favour this idea point out that this would link the various streams of development which currently penetrate the North from separate southern sources. They argue that it would connect the existing north-south transportation corridors and so provide a more complete transport network. This would in turn improve the access to known and possible new resources and spawn a new generation of towns in the "Near North." It is doubtful, however, whether these improvements in access would be sufficiently great to attract new enterprises away from the large established urban centres in the south.

THREE

What Cities Are For

1.   Introduction

In Part One we mentioned the idea of the functions of cities, that is, the idea that a city has a distinctive set of economic activities which is the basis of the city's existence. As examples we discussed briefly a forest products town and a fishing settlement. In Part Two we saw also that functions may change over time, and that some towns developed distinctive functions at various times in Canadian history. Quebec was principally a fortress, Montreal a port, Winnipeg a rail centre, and so on.

But what of urban centres today? The map of most populated areas is dotted with villages, towns, and cities, all of which have some reason for being where they are. If they served no function, then obviously they would soon cease to exist. In fact, many aspects of an urban centre's life may be traced back to its functions. A school, for example, is supported by taxpayers who make their incomes in the industries of the urban centre in which the school is located. In this section, therefore, we shall examine the idea of urban functions in some detail.

2.   Mining Towns

A few urban centres, generally small ones in rather remote locations, are so dominated by one function or economic activity that we can call them *single-function* towns. The classic example of such a single-function town is the *mining town,* a settlement located near some important mineral deposit, whose main

Fig. 3-1 Aerial view of Britannia Beach, B.C.

activity concerns the working of the mineral, the initial processing of the mineral, and its shipment to other centres for further use. Figure 3-1 shows an aerial view of such a town in British Columbia and Table 3-1 shows its labour force. We can see from the latter that though most people are employed in mining it is not the sole occupation.

Table 3-1   **Population and Employment in Britannia Beach, B.C. (1969)**

Population: 709
Employment:

       Anaconda Mine and Mill
         280 employees
           90 office workers
       1 general store
       1 cafe
       1 gas station
       1 post office
       1 elementary school
       1 customs office

1. In the photograph, identify the structures and buildings associated with mining activities. Is it possible to guess the specific mineral being mined here?
2. What other economic activities are probably carried on in this settlement, from the evidence of the photograph?
3. Express the mine and mill employment figures in Table 3-1 as percentages of the total town population. Estimate employment in the other economic activities in the settlement. What proportion of the total town population is this estimate?
4. Who are the likely customers of the stores and service businesses shown in the table?
5. What are the potential problems of a centre with an industrial structure like that of Britannia Beach?
6. What evidence is there in the photograph that the level of economic activity was once greater than it is now?

Besides mining activities, the town also has retailing activities, service businesses, educational and government activities, and so on. But clearly mining is the most important single activity in the town, the one that directly supports most families, and most significantly, the activity that is the main reason for the existence of the town. In other words, mining is the *town-forming* activity here; the other activities are essentially *town-serving*, that is, they exist to provide local services to the mining population and to one another. Thus we could say that in both a direct and indirect fashion, mining is the foundation of the whole economy of the town. It supports many families directly, while these in turn support many service businesses, and the families of service workers, indirectly. In these circumstances, the whole prosperity of the town is tied to the vitality of the town-forming activity, mining. If this declines (as it might well do, if the mineral is exhausted or if its price declines in world markets), then the whole economy of the town collapses. We have all heard of ghost-towns – communities abandoned by their populations after the collapse of their basic town-forming activities. This is a fate all single-function towns fear, but especially mining towns, since their prosperity is based on an *exhaustible resource,* a mineral deposit that can be used up. Many mining towns are literally undermining their own long-range future, even as they carry out their current activities.

TOWN SPIRIT WON'T GIVE UP GHOST

WELLS, B.C. This tough little town has been hit hard by impending closure of Cariboo Gold Quartz Mines – it's not going to die without a fight.

Though its heyday is long gone, Wells isn't ready to become a ghost town like its famous neighbor, Barkerville.

... The shadow of mine closure has long been cast over Wells, and there are many grim reminders of what may come, huddled behind eight-foot snowbanks along the main street.

There is the "Hill Meat Market," front windows smashed by snowblocks, a sign proclaiming mockingly "Open Every Wednesday," while the cold wind whistles over ruined counters.

Another derelict building has a fancy, faded sign, "G. W. Electric Ltd."; another, its glass front replaced by a rough latticework of boards, is identified simply as "MacKenzie's." There are other signs of decay, but many are due to the rumours of mine closure and the mine company's reluctance to spend money on the many buildings it owns.

Most of the mine employees who will soon lose their jobs have little else to lose. Experienced miners are always in demand in B.C., and some of the older men will simply retire here on their old age pension. Only the men too young to retire and too old to readily get work elsewhere, are worried.

... George Gilbert, co-manager of the mine, has lived in Wells since his eighth birthday. He isn't worried about getting another job although he is reluctant to leave the town.

"Death is always sad," he said "whether it comes to a person or a mine. This may cut Wells down to 200 people – but it'll come back. Wait and see."

Vancouver Province, February 16, 1967.

---

7. Locate Wells, B.C., on a map. Why have many stores closed? What may the displaced population of this town do as the town faces decay?
8. Using other sources, identify other single-function towns, especially mining towns that face decline because of the decay of their basic activity What can be done about this problem?

Because of the vulnerability of single-function towns, and especially mining towns, they face problems such as the emigration of young people to larger cities with more job opportunities, or problems of psychological insecurity on the part of people who stay. Public officials and business leaders in such towns are always anxious to attract new industry to the town to *diversify* the town's economy, and to provide alternative jobs against the possibility that the original supporting activity may some day decline. They may be helped in this by federal government policies, such as the Area Development Program, which gives financial help to new private firms setting up business in economically vulnerable centres.

3. Service Centres in Agricultural Regions

A second kind of single-function town is the service centre in an agricultural region. Many of the small towns across Canada fall into this category. The main town-forming activity of such centres has to do with the provision of services to the farmers of the surrounding region – collecting the farm produce for shipment to larger centres, selling and repairing agricultural equipment, selling factory goods to the farmer, and providing professional, personal, and government services to the farm family.

Fig. 3-2 Aerial view of Davidson, Sask.

9. Find Davidson on Figure 4-7. In the photograph, in Figure 3-2, identify the structures and buildings associated with the provision of services to farmers.
10. What other economic activities are probably carried on in this centre, from the evidence of the photograph?

Again, we always find in such centres a number of town-serving activities also, that is, stores and service businesses serving the population of the town itself. In this type of town, however, the distinction between town-serving and town-forming activities is a little hard to make, since both are of the same character; that is, they are service businesses. The essential point is that the town-forming businesses are of the type that cater to the farming population of the area around the town, the town-serving businesses serve mainly the population of the town itself.

Table 3-2   Population and Business in Davidson, Sask.

Population of Davidson in 1968	1,100
Population of area within a 25-mile radius	7,041

Total Business and Professional Services

	No.		No.		No.
Apparel and accessories Group		Food and Beverage Group		Other Groups	
Children's Wear	–	Bakeries	1	Barber Shops	2
Family Clothing Stores	–	Eating Places	4	Beauty Parlours	2
Jewellery Stores	1	Eating Places with		Billiard Parlours	1
Ladies' Wear	–	Beverage	1	Bowling Alleys	1
Men's Wear	–	Grocery Stores	2	Drug Stores	1
Shoe Stores	–	Locker Plants	1	Dry Cleaners	1
Tailors	–	Meat Markets	2	Egg Grading Stations	–
Automotive Group		Supermarkets	–	Electrical Contractors	3
Body Repair Shops	1	Furniture, Appliances and		Florists	–
Implement Dealers	3	Radio Group		Funeral Parlours	1
Motor Vehicle Dealers	2	Electrical Appliances	2	Hatcheries	–
Service Stations	5	Furniture Stores	1	Laundries	–
Bulk Oil Dealers	5	TV and Radio Repairs	2	Machine Shops	2
Building Materials and		Professional		Painters and Decorators	2
Hardware Group		Accountants	–	Plumbing and Heating	2
Building Contractors	2	Chiropractors	–	Photographers	–
Hardwares	2	Dentists	2	Printers	1
Lumber Yards	2	Medical Doctors	2	Road Contractors	–
Woodworking	1	Lawyers	2	Shoe Repairs	1
General Merchandise Group		Optometrists	–	Upholsterers	1
Catalogue Sales Offices	–	Veterinarians	1	Theatres	1
Department Stores	1	Grain Elevators			
General Stores	1	Number	7		
		Capacity 1,000,000 bu.			

SOURCE: Saskatchewan Industry Department, Area and Trade Development Branch.

11. In the list of businesses in Table 3-2, which do you think are mainly town-forming and which town-serving? Give the reasons for your opinion.
12. What might be the potential problems of such a town?

The area around the agricultural service centre, containing the farmers who support the town by their purchases of town goods and services, is sometimes called the *market area* of the town. (We shall find out more about the market areas of towns in Part Four.) One problem of the agricultural service centre is that its prosperity is based upon the size and prosperity of the population that supports it – the agricultural population of its market area. If the agricultural population of the town's market area should fall in numbers, or lose income, then the prosperity of the agricultural service centre itself is threatened, since, like the mining town, it has no alternative economic activity to support it.

Table 3-3   Changes in Urban Centres in Saskatchewan, 1951-1961

Overall Changes	No.	%
No. of centres at start of period	892	100
No. of centres emerging during period	16	1.8
No. of places disappearing during period	129	14.5
No. of centres declining during period	148	16.6
No. of centres at end of period	779	

Change in Types of Centre			
Type of Centre	No. in 1951	No. in 1961	% Change
Smallest centres	624	554	
Medium size centres	258	214	
Largest towns	10	11	
	892	779	—12.7%

SOURCE: G. Hodge, "Urban Systems and Regional Policy," *Canadian Public Administration,* IX (1966).

13. How can you explain the decline in the total number of urban centres in this region in this period? Calculate the change in the number of centres in the three classes of Saskatchewan centres over the period as percentages. How do you explain the particular decline of the smaller villages and towns compared to the larger towns of Saskatchewan?
14. Find out what happened to the total population of Saskatchewan in this period. If it increased, how do you reconcile this with the decline in the number of settlements?

In the Prairie provinces, for example, the number of agricultural service centres has been declining as the mechanization of agriculture and the uncertain prosperity of agriculture forces people of the farms into the big cities. As the prairie farm population falls, the number of small urban centres serving them falls also.

You can probably think of single-function towns other than mining towns and agricultural service centres – for example, fishing centres, logging centres, recreational resorts, tourist and administration centres. All might be expected to share – in their own ways – the problems inherent in dependence on a narrow economic foundation.

4.   Cities With Many Functions

Most cities, and all larger cities, have a range of economic functions. Generally, the larger a city, the more *diversified* is its economic structure, that is, the greater is the variety of economic activities represented there. Such cities may be said to be multi-functional.

Table 3-4   Employment in Selected Canadian Cities, 1961

	Metro. Halifax	Metro. Edmonton	Metro. Hamilton	Metro. Vancouver	Metro. Toronto	Metro. Montreal
Agriculture	141	1,346	4,116	3,806	6,524	3,970
Forestry	25	129	36	2,518	277	217
Fishing	150	23	62	1,836	82	41
Mines, etc.	66	2,839	287	1,581	1,737	1,052
Manufacturing (processing)	1,817	6,534	20,688	25,974	22,911	27,637
Manufacturing (fabricating)	5,655	10,943	40,402	31,511	211,600	227,744
Construction	3,373	12,442	10,585	19,897	51,055	56,310
Transport and Communication	7,667	14,649	9,374	34,934	68,701	88,634
Wholesale Trade	4,088	10,648	6,429	22,757	49,594	43,394
Retail Trade	8,344	17,062	17,599	37,142	96,902	85,029
Finance & Insurance	2,988	5,467	4,969	15,918	52,338	41,984
Education, Health & Welfare	7,865	15,135	13,185	30,941	61,067	68,999
Business Services	1,059	2,875	2,368	7,898	26,422	18,322
Personal Services	4,657	9,248	9,685	22,741	57,868	56,574
Other Services	1,934	3,809	3,592	8,800	22,365	23,053
Fed. & Provincial Admin.	20,695	11,210	2,272	10,512	23,851	21,904
Local Admin.	1,286	4,001	3,166	7,491	19,107	20,146
Unspecified	1,143	3,216	2,822	8,502	17,250	21,961
Total Employment	72,953	131,576	151,637	294,759	789,651	806,973

SOURCE: Dominion Bureau of Statistics, *Census of Canada* (Ottawa: Queen's Printer, 1961).

15. Express the figures in Table 3-4 as percentages of total city employment. What are the most important activities in each city? Does any particular activity dominate the city economy? Which are the most diversified cities?
16. What are the advantages of this diversification of the economy of the city?

The economic mix of a large city often includes resource extraction and processing, manufacture of goods for sale in distant areas, provision of services for the agricultural or small town population of the surrounding market area, administration of public services for this area, and so on. In addition, larger towns have manufacturing industries producing goods for the local town population itself (food industries, for example) and businesses providing services for the local town population. In other words, the variety of town-forming activities, on which the town depends for its prosperity, is wider, and the superstructure of town-serving activities is more elaborate in larger towns. This situation gives larger towns important benefits. For example, with a wide range of town-forming activities, a decline in any one of them does not necessarily mean economic decline for the whole town; other industries may be in a growth period and will support the town economy. At the same time workers displaced from declining industries can find new jobs in other industries in the same town, and do not have to migrate elsewhere for new jobs. Also, the variety of town-serving industries, by offering a range of facilities to industrial firms, commercial businesses, and workers, makes the larger town attractive to even

Fig. 3-3 Aerial view of downtown Montreal and waterfront

more new activity and population, and the town continues to grow and diversify. In other words, large, economically diversified towns are economically more stable than small specialized towns, are centres of immigration of businesses and of population, and tend to experience steady rates of growth.

17. In the photograph of Montreal shown in Figure 3-3, what functions would you say are represented by the buildings labelled A, B, C, D, and E?
18. What other functions can you see represented in the photograph?
19. Which of the functions identified are predominantly town-forming and which are town-serving?
20. What indications are there that there has been a change over a period of time in Montreal's functions? In particular, which functions would you say are increasing rapidly from the evidence available?
21. Which functions support each other, and which are not closely related?
22. Refer to Table 3-4. Which of Montreal's functions indicated by the city's employment figures are not found in the area shown by the photograph? Suggest why.
23. Make a table showing the labour force for your own home town. Is yours a single-function or a multi-function town? What basis do you have for your opinion?

One means that is often used to indicate the relative importance of any one economic activity in a city is the *location quotient*. This is, very simply, the ratio of the percentage of workers in a particular activity in a particular city, over the percentage of workers in that same activity for Canada as a whole. Thus, if 25 per cent of Vancouver's and 7 per cent of Canada's labour force are employed in the forest industry, then Vancouver's location quotient for that industry is 25/7 or 3.6. Thus the larger a city's location quotient is for a particular industry, then the greater is the city's importance in that industry. Thus, the location quotients identify the particular functional specializations of a city. A city with one or two high location quotients (over 2) is specialized in those few functions; a city with several medium location quotients (1 to 2) has a more diversified (multi-functional) economy. Table 3-5 shows location quotients for a number of metropolitan areas across Canada.

24. Put the cities in order according to the value of their highest location quotients. How would you interpret and account for the rank of each?
25. What similarities do you notice among those cities with the lower location quotients?
26. Plot the cities on an outline map of Canada, differentiating between those for which the highest location quotient is greater than 3.0, between 2.0 and 2.9, and less than 2.0. Account for the distributions.
27. List the cities which have:
    a) four location quotients of at least 1.5
    b) three location quotients of at least 1.5
    c) two location quotients of at least 1.5
    d) one location quotient of at least 1.5
    Which of the cities could be considered the most multi-functional from this evidence?

Table 3-5   Location quotients for selected Metropolitan Areas, 1961

Metropolitan area	Industry groups showing the four highest location quotients			
	Highest	2nd highest	3rd highest	4th highest
Calgary	Mines, quarries, oil wells (3.4)	Storage (2.7)	Wholesale trade (2.0)	Finance, insurance and real estate (1.4)
Edmonton	Wholesale trade (1.8)	Public administration and defence (1.5)	Services to business management (1.4)	Construction industry (1.4)
Halifax	Public administration and defence (4.0)	Health and welfare services (1.4)	Communication (1.4)	Wholesale trade (1.2)
Hamilton	Fabricating industries in manufacturing (1.9)	Other manufacturing (1.8)	Health and welfare services (1.1)	Retail trade (1.1)
Kitchener	Other manufacturing (2.3)	Fabricating industries in manufacturing (1.8)	Finance, insurance and real estate (1.4)	Retail trade (1.1)
London	Health and welfare services (1.9)	Finance, insurance and real estate (1.7)	Fabricating industries in manufacturing (1.3)	Wholesale trade (1.2)
Montreal	Fabricating industries in manufacturing (1.9)	Services to business management (1.5)	Finance, insurance and real estate (1.5)	Transportation (1.3)
Ottawa	Public administration and defence (4.5)	Communication (1.4)	Finance, insurance and real estate (1.3)	Services to business management (1.1)
Quebec	Public administration and defence (1.9)	Health and welfare services (1.5)	Other services (1.3)	Education and related services (1.2)
Saint John	Wholesale trade (1.9)	Health and welfare services (1.8)	Transportation (1.7)	Communication (1.5)
St. John's	Health and welfare services (2.0)	Public administration and defence (2.0)	Transportation (1.7)	Wholesale trade (1.7)
Sudbury	Mines, quarries, oil wells (17.0)	Health and welfare services (1.1)	Retail trade (1.0)	Education and related services (0.9)
Toronto	Services to business management (2.2)	Finance, insurance and real estate (1.9)	Fabricating industries in manufacturing (1.8)	Wholesale trade (1.4)
Vancouver	Storage (2.2)	Services to business management (1.8)	Finance, insurance and real estate (1.5)	Health and welfare services (1.4)
Victoria	Public administration and defence (3.5)	Health and welfare services (1.6)	Education and related services (1.3)	Retail trade (1.2)
Windsor	Fabricating industries in manufacturing (3.0)	Services to business management (1.3)	Education and related services (1.2)	Other services (1.2)
Winnipeg	Storage (3.3)	Wholesale trade (1.8)	Transportation (1.5)	Finance, insurance and real estate (1.5)

SOURCE: Leroy O. Stone, *Urban Development of Canada* (Ottawa: Queen's Printer, 1967), pp. 190-191.

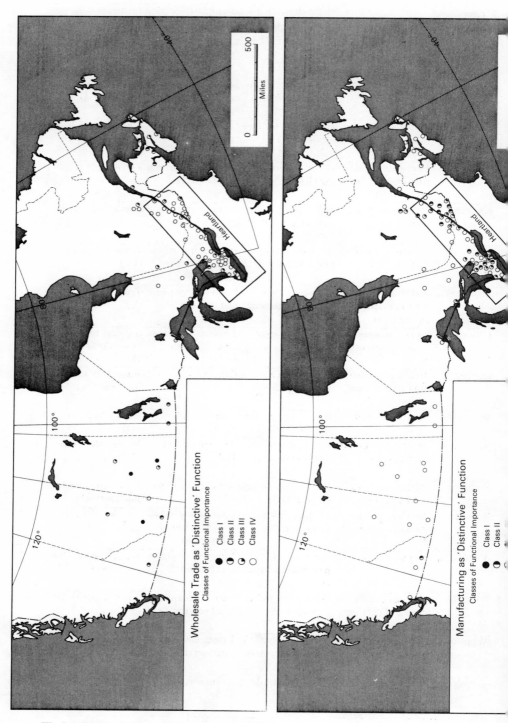

Fig 3-4 Distinctive functions of Canadian cities

There are obviously difficulties involved in trying to classify towns. One is the *multiple-function* problem. Many towns have a variety of economic functions but no distinctive functions, and cannot easily be put in one category. Montreal has manufacturing, wholesaling, and recreational functions; into which group is it to be placed? To call it a "manufacturing city" is to obscure its other functions. Classification may thus hide some of the characteristics of multi-function cities, and mislead us about the true nature of the cities it is supposed to be describing. One way out of this difficulty is to have a special category of "diversified cities," for cities without a clear functional character. A second difficulty in classification is that of deciding how narrow the classification will be. One can put the cities of a nation into a few broad categories (manufacturing cities, wholesaling cities, recreation centres, and so on) but one can also change the scale of classification, and, for example, divide the manufacturing class into smaller groups such as heavy manufacturing or light manufacturing towns. Increasing the number of classes in this way gives us more accurate descriptions of the towns, but makes the classification itself more cumbersome. These difficulties in classifying towns mean that there is no one correct classification of the towns of a nation. We could make several different functional classifications of the cities of Canada, and none of them would be the correct grouping. Each one would be only a more or less illuminating shorthand description of the function of Canadian cities, useful for particular purposes.

Although functional classification of this sort is thus never final, it can be useful. It reduces the numerous cities of a nation to a few groups and shows us the economic structure of the nation more clearly.

---

28. Locate and identify a few of the cities in Figure 3-4. What are the distinctive functions of (a) Hamilton, (b) Winnipeg, (c) Vancouver, (d) Saint John, (e) Regina, (f) Sherbrooke?
29. Explain the location of cities with different distinctive functions.

One approach to this question of city functions is taken in Figure 3-4. It identifies the importance of different kinds of functions for all the larger cities in Canada, rather than putting each city into a single functional class. The maps show that the cities in which manufacturing tends to be a distinctive function are concentrated in the Canadian *economic heartland,* the area of southern Ontario closest to the American manufacturing belt, where the consumer market is large and labour and capital are abundant. The cities in which wholesaling is the distinctive function are the large cities of the *economic fringe* of Canada, the areas where resource extraction and agriculture are more important than the fabrication of goods, and where cities tend to be collection and distribution centres, not production centres.

5.   The Economic Base Model

Earlier, we called the distinctive and important activities that support the economy of a town the town-forming activities, and the activities that exist mainly to provide goods and services to the town itself town-serving activities. Other terms for town-forming activities are the *economic base* of the town (*or basic activities*) and for town-serving activities the *service sector* (or *non-basic activities*). The distinction between the basic and non-basic activities of a town is fundamental to the examination of the functions of any town in terms of the so-called *economic base model* of the urban economy. The word "model" here is used as a social scientist would use it, to mean a simplified representation of some rather complicated situation. By reducing complex problems to their essential parts we may begin to understand them better. We shall discuss several "models" of different aspects of the city; for example, the urban economy, as here, or the spacing of towns or urban land use in later sections. Models are summaries of what we know about the world, and starting points for further exploration of problems. As our knowledge of the city increases, our urban models will become better (more realistic) but also more complicated. Most of the models mentioned in this book are rather simple, but they do help us to understand the way the real world works.

The economic base model is therefore an attempt to understand the urban economy. It divides the economic activities of a town into two components, basic and non-basic activities. To be precise, basic activities involve the sale of goods and services to customers outside the city itself. The firms which do this are exporters and bring money into the city. Part of the money earned by firms and workers in the basic sector is re-spent within the city, on locally-produced goods and services. The local firms that provide these goods and services actually make up the non-basic sector of the city economy. In other words, non-basic firms make most of their sales to customers within the city itself, not outside it. The entire urban economy, though, is considered supported by the exporting firms of the basic sector in this model. Figure 3-5 is a diagrammatic representation of this situation.

30. How else may income earned by firms in the basic sector be dispersed, other than by spending on locally-produced goods and services?
31. What will happen to the city economy if the amount of income earned by the basic sector grows?
32. What will happen to the city economy if the markets in which it sells its basic products contract with or are captured by a rival producer?

An important point about this model: it suggests that if the basic sector expands, and brings more money into the city (as it might, if the demands for the goods it produces increases in outside areas), then the whole city economy will grow. Extra money will be available in the city to support more non-basic service businesses also. Thus, growth in the basic sector causes the whole city to grow by encouraging more growth in the non-basic sector. This is called the *multiplier*

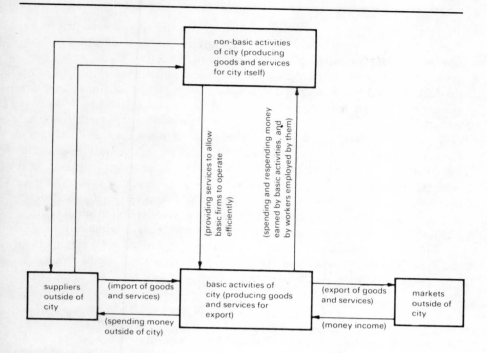

Fig. 3-5 Economic base model.

effect, since one sort of growth "multiplies" through the city to create more growth. This multiplier effect is particularly effective if little of the income earned by basic firms leaves the city to buy imports, that is, if most of it is spent again in the local area. This is actually the case with larger towns and is another reason why larger towns tend to have better records of economic growth than small ones.

Figure 3-5 shows that some of the income earned by basic activities may actually be spent outside of the city itself, that is, used to buy imports. This diagram illustrates well the fact that no city stands alone in economic terms. Every city is connected to other cities and places, since it exports to other cities the output of its own basic activities, and imports from other places a wide range of goods and services. These connections between the cities of a modern nation enable us to talk about the *urban system* of a nation. In an urban system, each city is more or less specialized in the production of some goods and services, and also all cities are *interdependent,* that is, depend on each other to be the markets for some of their exports, and the sources of some of their imports. For example, in Canada the smaller cities of the economic fringe extract and process resources that are often shipped to particular cities in the economic heartland for incorporation into manufactured goods. These manufactured goods are then distributed to consumers in other heartland cities, or in the fringe, through the chain of cities that have distributive functions. In short, specialized cities are linked to one another in an interdependent system by the exchange of materials, goods, and money.

However, many centres in an urban system are not only interdependent but are also *competitive;* they produce similar goods and services and try to sell them in the same markets. For example, many of the basic industries of Vancouver and Calgary compete for the custom of Western Canada; to a certain extent the growth of one centre is at the expense of other less successful centres that cannot hold and enlarge their outside markets as well. The competitive success of the basic industries of a town may depend on the relative advantage a town has due to a good location or may be connected with a skilled or energetic population. Also, the basic industries of large towns have distinct advantages when competing for markets since the elaborate service businesses of the larger towns tend to reduce the costs of operations of firms located there, and since the concentration of talented workers in larger places helps foster improvements in products or production processes. This competitive edge is another reason for the economic vitality of larger towns in comparison to small centres, and for the increasing concentration of population into larger urban centres.

The economic base of a particular city can be identified if we can discover the location of the customers of the various urban firms. The firms that sell to out-of-town customers are the basic firms.

33. On the evidence of Table 3-6 what are the basic manufacturing industries in Vancouver, and what are the non-basic industries?

34. In what markets does Vancouver probably sell the output of its basic industries? What centres would be its competitors? What advantages does Vancouver have for maintaining or increasing its sales while competing for markets?

Table 3-6   Proportion of Sales Made Outside of Vancouver Metropolitan Area by Selected Industries

Industry	Percentage of Sales (Rank Order)
Plywood and Veneers	89
Fish Processing	87
Industrial Machinery & Electrical Apparatus and Supplies	84
Sawmill Products	77
Iron & Steel Products and Non-Ferrous Metal Products (excl. Industrial Machinery)	60
Petroleum Products	55
Textile Products	55
Fruit & Vegetable Processing	51
Wood Products (other than Plywood & Veneers & Sawmill Products)	49
Paper Products	48
Chemical Products	44
Transport Equipment	36
Food & Beverages other than Fish, Fruit & Vegetables & Dairy Products	35
Non-Metallic Mineral Products	35
Dairy Products	12

Source: P. McGovern, "Industrial Development in the Vancouver Area," *Economic Geography* (1961), p. 205.

35. What kinds of manufactured goods does Vancouver probably import, and from where?
36. Using Table 3-6, is it possible to *clearly* assign all urban industries to the basic or non-basic categories?

For Vancouver, basic manufacturing clearly includes the plywood, fish, machinery, and sawmill industries, since these all sell over 75 per cent of their output outside of the metropolitan area. Industries such as the food and beverage industry sell most of the goods they produce to customers inside Vancouver itself, and can be called non-basic. However, the table also indicates a range of industries that are not clearly basic or non-basic, that is, they produce for both outside and local markets. These mixed cases indicate that in reality we must think of a city's industries as being more or less basic, and not rigidly *either* basic *or* non-basic, as the original simple economic base model seemed to suggest.

Despite the difficulties of applying the base model in practice, it is a useful idea. It reminds us that the prosperity of a city is tied up with the vitality of its exporting sector, so that events right outside a city (for example, in the area where it sells its products) can affect the city's fortunes. For example, an economic recession in Japan would seriously affect the prosperity of all the small British Columbia towns whose economic base involves producing coal, metal concentrates, and pulp for sale to Japanese industries. It also reminds us that a nation's cities today are highly interconnected, buying and selling goods and services from one another, related by bonds of interdependence and competition.

FOUR

Cities and Their Regions

1.   Introduction

Geographers use the word "region" in two quite different ways. Traditionally, areas which have a uniform climate, geology, natural vegetation, land use or some other feature have been called regions. The Canadian Shield is a region of this kind, and so are the Prairies, the Ontario Tobacco Belt, the Arctic, and so on. All are examples of what geographers call *homogeneous* regions since they contain at least one feature which is considered to be relatively homogeneous throughout the area defined as a region. Regions of this type may in fact be distinguished within cities, as in the areas of similar land use which we shall discuss in Part Five.

In this section, however, we are going to turn our attention to a different kind of region, which depends not upon the homogeneity of its separate parts but upon the fact that they are all connected to a central point in some way. One dictionary definition of the word "node" is a "central point of a system" and so regions of this kind are termed *nodal regions*. A nodal region then is one which is organized in some way about a central point, or node. The concept of the nodal region is a very useful one for organizing our ideas about activities which take place within and between urban centres.

What do we mean when we speak of the "Toronto Region"? Obviously we mean an area which falls in some way within the influence of Toronto. But in *what* way? Just as the extent and boundaries of homogeneous regions depend entirely on the feature we have chosen to distinguish them *as* regions, then so do the boundaries and extent of nodal regions such as the "Toronto Region" depend upon a similar choice of criteria. The features we choose to distinguish homogeneous regions usually have fixed locations, like the geology, the natural vegetation, or land use. The features we choose to distinguish nodal regions, on the other hand, are usually concerned with movement in some way. Consequently, nodal regions are much more likely than homogeneous regions to fluctuate and change through time.

2.   Nodal Regions Inside and Outside Cities

Two examples may help to make the concept of the nodal region a little clearer, one concerned with the relationships which exist within a city and the other with those relationships which tie a city in some way to other parts of the country.

One very obvious relationship which exists within cities is the link between the home and the office. During the morning and evening rush hours the streets, buses, subways, and other transport facilities are filled with *commuters* travelling between home and work, the resulting congestion often posing serious problems both for the commuters themselves and for city planners. From one point of view, we could regard each workplace as a node and the area containing the homes of its employees as the nodal region based upon it.

Figure 4-1 shows an example of such a nodal region. The small square indicates the location of the Hudson's Bay Company department store in downtown Vancouver, the dots the locations of the homes of one in every five of the people that work there.

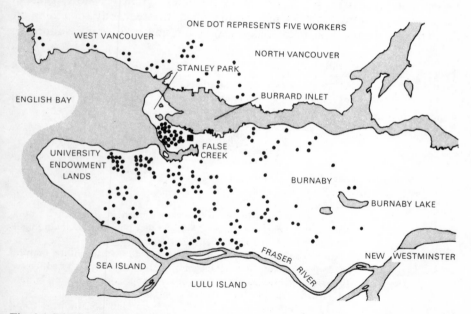

Fig. 4-1 Distribution of the homes of employees of the Hudson's Bay Company department store in Vancouver

1. Show the "commuting region" of the Hudson's Bay Company store by joining the store to each of the homes shown by a straight *flow line*. From which direction do most commuters come? Why might this information be of interest to city planners?
2. Would the information provided by Figure 4-1 be sufficient to plan the transportation needs of downtown Vancouver? If not, what additional sources of information might be needed?

3. What factors might explain the uneven distribution of the homes of the Hudson's Bay Company employees?

4. In addition to the "commuting region" a "customer region" might be drawn for the department store. How could data for a map showing a customer region be collected? What purpose might such a map serve?

5. Plot a map showing the "student region" of your class or school. What factor affects the distribution of students but does not affect the distribution of either employees or customers of the department store?

The concept of the nodal region may be used not only to organize our ideas about movements within cities but also about movements between cities. In Part One we discussed the hinterlands of ports and in Part Two the market areas of agricultural service centres. Both hinterlands and market areas are examples of nodal regions, for there is movement between both and the urban centre on which they are based. We may take up the idea of the hinterland of a port in more detail, and expand on it. Goods converge on ports like Montreal, Halifax, and Vancouver for export overseas, while imports are in turn sent from each of these ports to Canadian destinations. Thus, each port has *both* an export and an import hinterland with which its various facilities – grain elevators, general cargo wharves, storage sheds – may be identified. Consequently something of the nature of the port's two hinterlands can be inferred from its appearance.

6. Vancouver's major exports are listed below.

asbestos	lumber and logs
coal	petroleum products
copper ore	potash
fertilizer	propane gas
canned fish	pulpwood chips and hog fuel
flour	sulphur
fodder and feed	tallow
grain	woodpulp
lead and zinc alloys	

a) From which point(s) in the sketch map shown in Figure 4-2 would each of these exports be shipped? Which other points on the map might be associated with imports rather than exports?

b) Using an economic atlas or other source, shade on an outline map of Canada the probable place of origin of each of the exports listed. Draw a line around these to show Vancouver's approximate export hinterland. How might this differ from the import hinterland?

7. What could be inferred about the export hinterland of Montreal from Figures 2-5 and 3-3?

8. Which of the following are homogeneous and which nodal regions? Suggest in each case the homogeneous feature, or the node.
   a) The Canadian Shield.
   b) The province of Quebec.
   c) The area served by the radio station CKEY-Toronto.
   d) The area from which customers come to Honest Ed's discount store in Toronto.
   e) The Maritime Region.

9. What other examples of nodal regions can you think of?

The idea of the nodal region is thus quite a general one in urban studies. In fact, a number of special words exist to define different sorts of nodal regions. It may be helpful to define these terms a little more clearly. Though originally the word "hinterland," which means in German "the land behind," was used only to refer to the area served by a port, it is often used today to refer to the area served by any town. Other terms which are also used to refer to the area served by a town include the *market area,* the *service area,* the *trading area,* or the *umland.* For the sake of simplicity, we shall refer in this book to the market or service areas of towns, the trading areas of stores, and the hinterlands of ports.

3.   Trading Areas — A Field Activity

From one point of view, the city consists of a mosaic of nodal regions centred upon particular points such as workplaces, stores, entertainment centres. Some of these regions, like the school district, are defined by an administrative decision: that is, the school board decides which areas are to be served by a particular school. Others are defined by the operation of free choice among a great number of individuals; for example, housewives choose the supermarket from which they will buy their groceries. In this case, we might expect most shoppers to prefer to go to the nearest supermarket, and thus the limits of the store trade area would be set by competition of stores for customers on the basis of convenience. There will always be a few people, however, who will happily travel halfway across town to patronize a store which they believe sells better meat, fresher vegetables, or has lower prices. There will also be those living near more than one supermarket who will not really care which one they patronize. As a consequence, the boundaries of the "customer regions" of supermarkets, or any other facility, are generally not strict lines but indeterminate zones, and the trade areas of stores will often overlap.

Figures 4-3 and 4-4 show two different kinds of grocery store similar to those which most of us pass or visit almost every day. In the one case we have a small neighbourhood grocery store, in the other, a chain supermarket located in a planned shopping centre. Although they both deal in essentially the same kind of produce, it is obvious that they are different in many ways.

10. What is a major difference between the residential areas in which each of the two stores is located? What conclusions might be drawn from this?
11. Which store probably carries the biggest inventory of stock? What conclusions might be drawn from this?
12. What evidence can be seen in the photograph to suggest that the supermarket draws customers from a more extensive area than the neighbour-

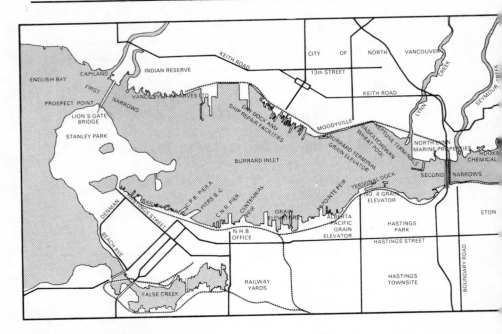

Fig. 4-2 The port of Vancouver

Fig. 4-3 A neighbourhood grocery store

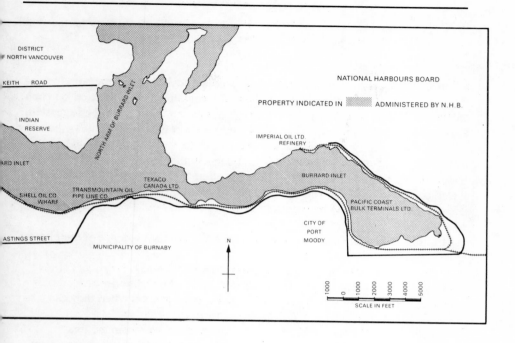

Fig. 4-4 A planned shopping centre with a chain supermarket

hood grocery store? What other kinds of retail stores might be found in the same shopping centre as the supermarket?

From the answers to these questions it should be possible to frame some tentative suggestions about the nature of the nodal region which is centred on each store – the trading area from which it draws its customers. It might be suggested, for example, that the trading area of the supermarket is bigger, because there is some evidence that people drive to it and walk to the neighbourhood grocery store. We might also go beyond this and suggest that customers are willing to travel further to the supermarket because it offers a greater choice of goods, has lower prices, gives them the opportunity of visiting other stores, and so on. These suggestions could be regarded as *hypotheses* about the trading areas of supermarkets and neighbourhood grocery stores.

Putting it another way, we could *hypothesize* from the evidence of the photographs that:

a) supermarkets have bigger trading areas than neighbourhood grocery stores;

b) customers drive to supermarkets and walk to neighbourhood grocery stores;

c) customers are willing to travel further to the supermarket when they can also visit other stores in the same shopping centre;

d) most customers come from close to the store, and fewer from far away.

The procedure we are following is that of any scientist investigating a problem – making a list of what we think may be true on the basis of the evidence available to us. The next task, of course, is to see whether our hypotheses can be verified by taking a look at some additional evidence, which might take the form of more photographs, collected data, or other sources. Since much geographical research involves field work, this is the procedure we are going to suggest here. By actually visiting stores like those shown in Figures 4-3 and 4-4 and observing or asking questions, we should be able to find out whether our hypotheses are true.

What we decide to do on a field trip to the stores would constitute our *research design* and might include activities such as observation, interviewing, or the administering of a questionnaire. Each of these tasks demands the development of special skills. In much field work, it is better if the load is shared among a group, and it is necessary that the consent of those you are studying is obtained.

13. Observe two selected stores for a fixed period at the same time each day. How many customers enter each store? By what means of transportation do they arrive?

14. Observe customers at the checkout of each store. How many articles are they purchasing? Of what kinds? What is the total bill?

15. Observe whether customers have shopping lists. What significance might the answer have?

16. Observe the time customers spend between entering and leaving each store and divide by the number of purchases they have made. Would the data have any implications for the argument over self-service versus service by a salesman?

17. Find out where advertised specials are located in the supermarket. Talk to the manager about the effect of advertising and try to reach an independent opinion by observing customers purchasing advertised specials.

18. By questioning a sample of customers, find out their home addresses (to the nearest block) and which other stores they have visited on the same shopping trip. Make a flow map from this data. Does it look like a trade area? How many of the customers come from within six blocks of the store? From within twelve blocks? More than twelve blocks?
19. Which of the activities suggested above depend on observation alone, which on interview, and which on the administering of a questionnaire?
20. Which are relevant to the hypotheses suggested on page 62?

Using the above discussion and questions as a guide, plan and carry out a field exercise which will help you find out as much as possible about the trading areas of a supermarket and a neighbourhood grocery store in your own locality. First, set up a number of hypotheses which you wish to investigate. Second, make a research design which will enable you to find out by field work whether your hypotheses are true. Third, map the supermarkets and neighbourhood grocery stores in your locality and decide which you want to investigate. Fourth, carry out the field work itself. Last and most important, discuss your results fully, deciding which hypotheses they answer and which further hypotheses they raise.

4.   Service Thresholds

In Part Three we saw that many urban centres exist by providing goods and services to the areas surrounding them, and that their principal function is that of service centre. For example, the small town shown in Figure 3-2 has the principal function of providing services to those who live in the surrounding agricultural area. Its general store, gas station, hardware store, and other facilities are patronized not only by the town's residents but also by the farming population who come into town from time to time. Without the support of both groups, most of these facilities would not be able to survive.

For any facility to survive (i.e., to operate profitably) it must be able to rely upon a certain minimum number of customers, a number which is called the *threshold population* or the *threshold market*. To illustrate the concept of the threshold, assume that we are going to open a dry goods store in the town of Jonesville in the imaginary example shown in Figure 4-5. For the sake of simplicity, suppose that the neighbouring towns labelled A, B, C, D, E, and F are each fourteen miles away, that each already has a dry goods store but Jonesville itself does not, that the population density of the rural area is 10 people per square mile, and that the population of Jonesville is 460. Suppose also that a population of at least 2000 is needed to support a dry goods store or, putting it another way, that 2000 is a dry goods store's threshold population.

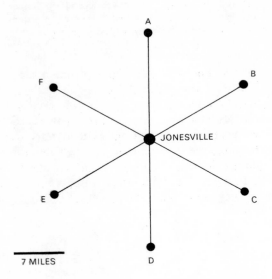

Fig. 4-5 Locations of imaginary towns containing dry goods stores

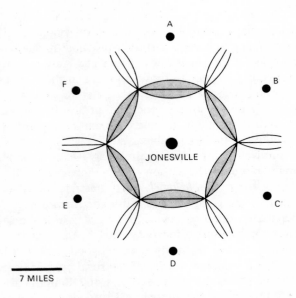

Fig. 4-6 Trading areas of the dry goods stores in each of the towns

21. Assuming that our store is only as good as, but no better than, the dry goods stores at each of the neighbouring towns, from how far away can we reasonably expect to draw our customers?

22. Using this value as a radius, what is the size of the area from which we could expect our customers to come? (The area of a circle is given by πr^2 where π is equal to $2\frac{2}{7}$.)

23. With a density of 10 people per square mile, what is the population of this area? Add this amount to the population of Jonesville itself to find the total population our store will serve. Will it survive? The answer, of course, is "yes" only if the total population is at least the threshold number of 2000.

24. What would the effect be upon our store if the neighbouring towns were only seven miles away?

25. What would the effect be if the population density increased, or if the population increased its spending power?

26. What might the effect be upon our competitors in the neighbouring towns if we made our store much better than theirs, and advertised?

If neither of the possibilities mentioned in the last two questions were to become actualities, then our store would continue to share the market with those in the neighbouring towns as shown in Figure 4-6. Our customers would come from a circle of seven miles' radius around Jonesville, and our competitors' customers would come from similar circles centred upon each of the neighbouring towns, on the principle of convenience mentioned earlier. If each of the stores really were no better than the others and all the towns were equally accessible, then the customers even in the shaded areas would be equally divided, so that the circles would assume the shape of regular hexagons.

Of course, the example we have looked at is unlikely to be found in real life since stores are rarely exactly the same, and neither are customers. However, this ideal type or model (see page 53) does allow us to understand something about the way the real world works, but without many of the complicating factors that the real world contains. For example, it helps us to understand why the populated parts of Canada are laced with a network of small towns, all containing approximately the same facilities. In places where the productivity of the land or the topography are varied the population density varies as well, and so these towns may not be numerous, nor are they spaced evenly. But, in more uniformly populated areas like parts of the Prairies or Southern Ontario, the actual network of service centres can approximate the model closely.

27. Assuming that each of the villages shown on the map in Figure 4-7 has roughly the same facilities, indicate on a piece of tracing paper overlaid on the map the ideal market areas of each village.

28. If you were able to do field work in the area, how might you verify whether your ideal construction applied? (You may find it helpful to look back at question 18.)

29. What factors might cause your ideal construction to be distorted in reality?

If we were interested in opening a furniture store rather than a dry goods store we should require a greater number of potential customers, since people generally buy furniture less frequently than they buy dry goods. While dry goods

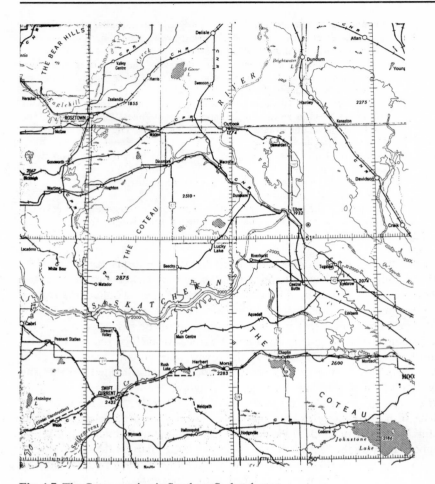

Fig. 4-7 The Coteau region in Southern Saskatchewan

stores may be said to enter an urban centre over a relatively low threshold, furniture stores are able to do so only over a much higher threshold. Small urban centres therefore have general stores, gas stations, restaurants, and dry goods stores, while larger ones have all of these things plus boutiques, hair stylists, ski shops, furniture stores, and many, many others. The really large centres like New York have populations which are so big that they contain enough potential customers for even the most specialized of services. If you are considering opening a store which sells wigs to balding poodles, you are more likely to be successful in New York than in Horsefly, B.C.!

The actual threshold of particular services is of interest to businessmen and planners alike and may be calculated with little difficulty if certain assumptions are made. If an area with 500 people has one general store, one with 1000 has two, and one with 1500 has three, it seems fairly certain that the population threshold for general stores would be 500 people. That is, it requires 500 people to support one general store. Table 4-1 gives populations and the numbers of a selection of different services found in a variety of towns in Ontario. In

Table 4-1 **Populations and numbers of selected services in Ontario cities with populations greater than 30,000 and less than 500,000**

City	Population	Movie Theatres	Pool Rooms	Barber Shops	Laundromats	Eating Places	Taverns	Auto Rentals	Driving Schools
Ottawa	494,535	15	17	239	36	366	37	9	7
Hamilton	449,116	15	38	280	49	278	46	8	7
Windsor	211,697	5	15	139	28	138	54	4	3
London	207,397	7	7	116	21	154	7	2	1
Kitchener	192,275	6	7	112	12	106	6	4	1
Sudbury	117,075	6	16	69	13	85	4	2	—
St. Catharines	109,418	4	8	85	11	69	9	4	2
Oshawa	100,255	5	6	62	10	63	—	2	1
Thunder Bay	97,770	4	14	58	8	86	6	3	—
Kingston	71,540	3	4	41	6	50	2	1	1
Sarnia	66,713	2	5	37	10	48	2	1	—
Brantford	62,036	2	5	43	9	31	5	2	1
Niagara Falls	60,768	2	5	45	3	73	10	1	1
Welland	59,152	3	10	46	7	41	7	1	1
Peterborough	56,177	2	2	42	9	36	4	—	—
Guelph	51,377	2	4	30	8	35	1	1	1
Cornwall	45,766	2	4	27	5	29	4	—	2
Brampton	45,168	1	2	18	6	16	—	3	—
Timmins	39,806	2	6	25	4	32	16	1	—
Belleville	32,785	2	3	20	5	26	—	3	1
Chatham	32,424	2	3	26	5	25	5	—	—

SOURCE: Dominion Bureau of Statistics, *Census of Canada*, 1966.

30. Using graph paper, plot graphs similar to Figure 4-8 for a selection of the other services given in Table 4-1. What are the estimated threshold populations for each of them? How do you account for the differences?

31. What are the population and the numbers of each service in your own town? (or, if you live in a large city where the figures are difficult to work with, in a moderately sized town known to you?) Plot the figures for one or two services on graphs.

32. What factors might cause the points for any particular town to lie either well above or well below the average line for each service?

33. What effect would it have upon the thresholds if we were able to take the population of the service areas of the towns into account?

Figure 4-8 data from the table are used to calculate a population threshold necessary to support a movie theatre. The population of each town has been plotted against the numbers of theatres in the town to give a series of points. If we were to draw a line roughly through these points and then project it back towards the vertical axis, an estimate of the population needed to support the

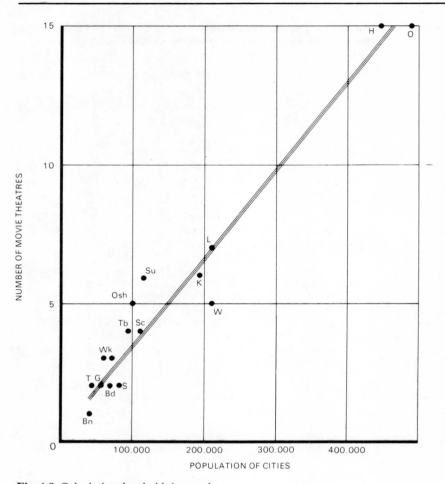

Fig. 4-8 Calculating thresholds by graphs

facility (the threshold population) could be made. If we assume the city population is the same as the city region population for these low threshold
examples, one movie theatre could survive in an urban centre with a population
of about 20,000.

5.   Village, Towns, and Cities

Goods and services which require only a low population threshold are said to be
of *low order*. A loaf of bread is a low order product and a haircut a low order
service since both are purchased frequently by a high proportion of the population. A Rolls Royce, on the other hand, is a very *high order* product since only
a very small proportion of the total population buys one and then not very often.
Similarly brain surgery is a high order service. It requires only a small population

then to contain enough potential purchasers of loaves of bread and haircuts (low order goods and services) to support a bakery and a barber. On the other hand, it requires a very large population to contain enough potential purchasers of Rolls Royces and brain surgery (high order goods and services) to support a Rolls Royce dealer and a hospital specializing in brain surgery.

If we wished, we could group all goods and services into high, intermediate, and low orders as shown below.

ORDER OF SERVICE

	High:	Intermediate:	Low:
City	department store, specialized hospital, theatre, etc.	furniture store, physician, laundromat, etc.	grocery store, gas station, barber, etc.
Town	none	same	same
Village	none	none	same

Generally speaking, we should find the high order services in cities, the intermediate order in towns, and the low order in villages. We expect to find general stores, gas stations, and other low order services in villages, but we might be surprised to find delicatessens or stores selling Scandinavian furniture. Most village regions just do not contain enough people to provide a sufficient number of customers to support such activities, while city regions do. Cities then might contain all the services listed on the table above, towns only those in the second and third columns, and villages only those listed in the third column.

34. In Figure 4-9, which street would you identify as containing generally high order stores? Which street would you say is more likely to be in a city rather than a small town? What evidence might you present for your opinion?

35. Ask the members of your class to make a list of the places where they or their family last purchased the following: a loaf of bread, a carton of milk, a can of vegetables, a packet of detergent, a pair of pants or a dress, a pair of shoes, a record, a TV set, a carpet, a car.
(List shopping centres if you live in a city and other urban centres if you live in a town or village.)
Calculate the average distance travelled for each article and try to explain the variation, if any.

Generally speaking, cities are few and far between while towns and villages are more numerous and closer together. Geographers have developed a theory to explain the spacing of cities, towns, and villages with reference to the kinds of services they contain. All urban centres, they suggested, are *central places* for some nodal region which they provide with goods and services. Just what kinds of goods and services depends upon the size of the central place and of the region it serves.

Fig. 4-9 Retail Streets

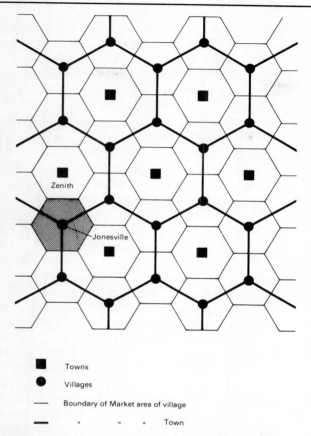

Towns

Villages

— Boundary of Market area of village

— "   "   " Town

Fig. 4-10 Market areas of towns and villages on an imaginary uniform plane

To see how the *Central Place Theory* was developed, let us return to the imaginary example used earlier to find whether a dry goods store could survive in a particular location (page 65). If we were to widen the field of view of Figures 4-5 and 4-6 we might find that our imaginary villages are just seven among a greater number of similar central places. Figure 4-10 shows how these might be spaced in order to provide services as efficiently as possible to the entire area shown on the map. If all the stores in each of the villages had approximately the same threshold as that of a dry goods store, then the hexagonal regions surrounding them would represent the market areas of the villages themselves. For example, all of the people living in the area shown by the shaded hexagon will go to Jonesville for all their low order goods and services. Consequently Jonesville could be regarded as a *low order central place*.

If no other villages existed than those shown then all the high order needs of those living in the area would go unsatisfied. Although they would be able to buy bread, milk, vegetables, and haircuts, there would be no town where they could buy clothes, shoes, records, television sets, furniture, and cars. In poor societies where effective demand is limited, there are often no larger centres which can provide high order goods and services, but in our own society this is not so.

Let us assume then that the town of Zenith is larger than its neighbours and contains high order facilities in addition to those found in the other villages. A furniture store in Zenith would only be able to survive if it drew its customers from a wider area than that served by the Zenith grocery stores, gas stations, and other low order facilities. The reason for this, as we have seen, is that people generally purchase furniture much less frequently than they purchase groceries and gas, and consequently a larger total population is required in order to provide enough potential furniture buyers at any one time for the furniture store to make a profit. Fortunately for the furniture store owners, because people do not buy furniture as often as groceries and gas they are prepared to travel farther to do so. For example, in question 35 you may have noted that your family's large purchases, like television sets and cars, were generally made farther from home than the smaller ones like bread and milk.

Let us say that the area enclosed by the heavy solid line in Figure 4-10 is large enough to contain a sufficiently big population to provide a furniture store and other stores of the same order with customers. We could say also that people would be prepared to come from as far away as the heavy solid line to purchase furniture. This distance is called the *range* of a furniture store, where the range of any goods or service is the maximum distance from which they will draw customers. Generally, the higher the order of goods or service, the higher also will be the range. That is, the less frequently you need to buy something then the farther you will be prepared to travel to do so. Large central places like Zenith then contain a greater number of goods and services of both high order and range and consequently serve bigger regions than the small central places like Jonesville. Zenith then is a higher order central place than Jonesville.

In our example, we have only considered two orders of central place, but in reality we know that there are many. In the real world, the largest cities like Montreal, Toronto, and Vancouver provide goods and services of very high order to enormous regions. Smaller cities like, say, Trois Rivières in Quebec, Stratford in Ontario, or Kamloops in British Columbia provide lower order goods and services to less extensive regions, while the smaller towns and villages provide quite small regions with their everyday needs. All fit together into a *hierarchy* of cities, towns, and villages such that most people in the country can reach urban centres of every order, and therefore are able to satisfy all their needs.

---

36. Draw a map of your local area showing the urban centres which you would consider to be of low, intermediate, or high order: i.e., villages, towns, and cities.

    Plan a research design which would enable you to find out whether the centres of higher order serve a more extensive region than those of lower order for a selection of services.

    Part of your research design, for example, might include interviewing selected store owners or medical or education officials to find out where their out-of-town clients come from.

37. What factors may have distorted the distribution of urban centres shown on your map from an ideal distribution like that shown in Figure 4-10?

---

6. Other Kinds of Urban Region

We have looked at urban centres mainly as places existing to provide goods and services which people living in the surrounding region purchase directly. In fact, urban centres are far more than just service centres. Most towns have a large number of different functions, many of which – the town-forming ones – connect the urban centre to the surrounding area. Money flows into the urban centre for services provided, but these services can include not only retailing services, but also administrative, medical, legal, educational, and many more. The precise limits of the regions served will be different for each of the services offered, which makes the drawing of nodal regions taking into account *all* of a city's functions difficult.

---

38. Identify in Figure 4-11 the buildings which are associated with the services Toronto provides for the surrounding area.
39. Try to put the services with which the buildings are associated into the order suggested by the size of the regions they serve.

Of course, your answers to the last question may be based upon guesswork, since we really have very little idea where the people come from who patronize the Royal Ontario Museum (in the right foreground), the Park Plaza Hotel (in the centre foreground), or from how far the University of Toronto draws its students, for example. Some of the buildings we know probably serve a very

Fig. 4-11 Aerial view of Toronto, looking south

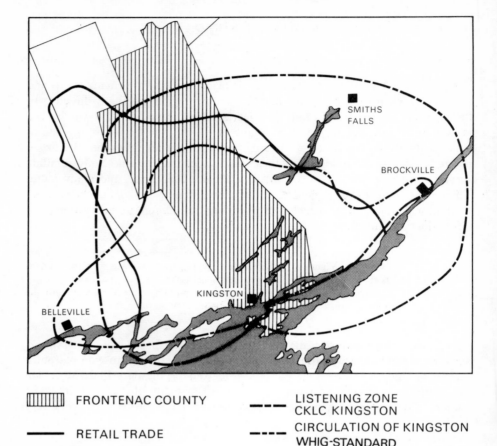

Legend	
▥ FRONTENAC COUNTY	--- LISTENING ZONE CKLC KINGSTON
▬ RETAIL TRADE	-·-·- CIRCULATION OF KINGSTON WHIG-STANDARD

Fig. 4-12 Some regions centred on Kingston, Ont.

local region like the church to the left of the Park Plaza Hotel, since the majority of its worshippers probably come from within Toronto itself. Other buildings we know serve regions of national or even international extent. Many of the tenants of the tall Toronto-Dominion Centre in the middle background conduct business all over the world as do the port facilities behind. What is important is that all provide services of quite different kinds to regions of quite different sizes.

Some of the buildings we can, of course, associate with very precisely defined regions. The Parliament Buildings in Queen's Park (at right centre) contain the administration for the region bounded by the political limits of the Province of Ontario. Thus Ontario itself is the region for which Toronto provides the kinds of administrative services associated with the Provincial Government. Administrative services are also provided by the City Hall (in the middle background) but they are provided only to the region contained by the limits of Metro Toronto.

Besides being a centre of administration, Toronto is also a communications centre. News and information go out from Toronto to all parts of the country so that, in this respect, its influence is felt everywhere in Canada. This influence is stronger closer to Toronto itself; how close depends upon the particular communications medium we are talking about. People living close to Toronto may listen to CHUM–Toronto, while those living as far away as Thunder Bay read more Toronto newspapers than Winnipeg ones. And so we could continue almost indefinitely. A large multi-functional city like Toronto provides a vast range of services of many kinds to regions of greater or lesser extent. If we wished to define the Toronto Region accurately we should have to take account of all these services, an obvious impossibility. With nodal regions, as with homogeneous regions, it is necessary to define a purpose for regionalization and to specify clearly the criteria upon which the region is based.

40. With what functions are each of the regions identified in Figure 4-12 associated?
41. In what ways have some of the regions been affected by the highway system?
42. In what ways are some affected by nearby centres?
43. What buildings might be found in Kingston which would be associated with the regions shown in Figure 4-12?
44. What other regions might be centered upon Kingston? List all of the regions in a table like the following.

Extent	Region	Function
Large		
Medium		
Small		

45. Construct a similar table for your own town or city and draw a map showing the different regions centred upon it.
46. What significant differences may be observed between the regions centred upon Toronto, Kingston, and your own town or city?

FIVE

Land Uses Within Cities

1.   Introduction

In this section we change focus once again to look at the differences which occur within cities rather than between cities. Thus we are now dealing with things at the *intra*-urban rather than the *inter*-urban level, as in most of the earlier sections. Just as geography has an interest in how cities, towns, and villages are spaced, and in the relationships which exist between them and their surrounding areas, so also it has an interest in the distributions of activities and people within cities, and connections which exist between one part of the city and another. This interest it shares also with other subjects, but geography's interest often begins with maps.

A city or town is a collection of activities of many kinds, as we found in Part Three. Most urban centres contain a mixture of industrial, financial, and retail uses, and all contain the homes of the people who work in and are served by these activities. Thus the map of every city shows a variety of *land uses,* or particular functions occupying a given area. At first glance, the land use map of a large city seems complex and confusing. However, when you know what to look for, *patterns* of land use emerge; the same patterns are repeated within many Canadian cities, and are the result of the operation of forces which sort out urban activities into typical locations.

For example, all large Canadian cities have a distinctive downtown area where certain kinds of financial and retail activities are concentrated. Industrial zones containing manufacturing, transport, and wholesale activities are found close to downtown, along waterfronts or railways. Most of the rest of the urban land area is given over to residential land uses, which can vary considerably, for example, the old dense residential areas near the centre of the city and the newer, less dense developments on the suburban edge. Dotted over the residential areas are commercial land uses, stores and service businesses serving the surrounding residential population. Roads, subways, and streetcar lines link these various activities and areas, and are themselves an important land use in the modern city. Also, open space for recreation and leisure use breaks up the work-a-day pattern of land use, in the form of golf courses, parks, and so on, as do the various institutional land uses like hospitals, defence installations, or university campuses. In the following pages we shall look at some of these land uses in more detail, and try to understand the basis of their location and character.

Fig. 5-1 Aerial view of downtown Calgary

2.   Downtown

First, we can consider the downtown area, perhaps the most distinctive and complex part of any Canadian city.

1. In the photograph shown in Figure 5-1 what characteristics distinguish downtown Calgary from the rest of the city?
2. Make a list of each type of land use that you can identify within the downtown area. Why should downtown be given over to these land uses?
3. Orient the photograph in Figure 5-1 with Figure 5-2. Identify on the map the bridge A on the photograph. What direction was the photographer facing?
4. Imagine that you are driving out of Calgary on any of the avenues coming towards you in the photograph. Draw a sketch map showing the land uses you would expect to pass in each city block along the way.
5. Using the map as a guide and the photograph as a source of information, draw a map of downtown Calgary showing the height of the buildings. Show those of over ten stories in a dark shade, those of between five and ten in a medium shade, and those of less than five in a light shade. What conclusions might be drawn from the distribution on your map?
6. What factors do you think might account for the heavy concentration of parking lots on the fringes of the downtown area?

Fig. 5-2 Map of downtown Calgary

7. What evidence can you see of changing land use both within the downtown area and on the fringes of downtown? Why might it be difficult to draw a precise boundary for the downtown area?

Downtown, or as it is sometimes called, the *central business district,* is distinctive in several respects. Its appearance is distinctive since tall buildings crowd together in a small space to create impressions of density and intensity of land use. Hundreds of people and cars throng the same small area and add movement and vitality to the downtown scene. The tall buildings reflect the high price of downtown land. As many firms compete for the use of downtown land, its price is driven up. Developers and firms erect tall buildings on small spaces to get the maximum earnings from their costly sites. Downtown is thus three-dimensional; it exists up in the air as well as over the ground.

This area is also distinctive in its functions. Retailing, recreation, and business are typical downtown activities. One part of downtown is a shopping district – possibly the main shopping area of the whole city – like Yonge Street in Toronto, Jasper Avenue in Edmonton, Portage Avenue in Winnipeg, or Granville Street in Vancouver. It contains department stores and specialty shops, the kind of stores that most people in the city visit sooner or later, and which therefore need to be in the centre of the city if they are to be accessible to most of the city population.

Recreational functions include cinemas, theatres, art galleries, and also the hotels which cater to the tourist population that every large city attracts. Often these activities are found close together and also close to the shopping district, as in Vancouver's Granville and Georgia Streets. Having these functions close together enables people to choose from the variety of facilities available, or to use both stores and entertainment facilities on the same downtown visit.

Business activities are often segregated in another section of downtown, sometimes near to public buildings such as the city hall or the law courts. This area of downtown is usually frantically busy by day but empty and quiet at night or on weekends. It has no residential population, since it has only a day-time function. Typically, these functions include the head offices of large cor-porations and also the many smaller firms – lawyers, accountants, consultants, advertisers and so on – that provide them with specialist services. Such activities crowd into the part of downtown that can be reached by public transport from broad areas of the city, from where they draw their labour force. These firms value the prestige of a downtown location, and so remain there despite the high rents they must pay and the problems of congestion caused by crowded streets. Most important, though, is that these business firms benefit from being close together; they may exchange business news and be able to react quickly to changing events. Thus all are committed to a downtown location together. Dotted through the financial district of a large city we also often find small stores and cafés that cater to the working population of the area during the working day.

Downtown is also the focus of the city transport system. Freeways, bus lines, and rail tracks converge on it. This is not surprising given that hundreds of people want to travel downtown every day to work, to shop, or for recreation. But it also means that downtown is highly accessible from most other places in the city. And this explains in fact why those specialized stores and businesses, which need to be able to serve people in all parts of the city to survive, continue to operate from a downtown location.

---

8. For what reasons may the following activities be located in the downtown area: (a) a department store; (b) a lawyer's office; (c) a high quality jewellery store; (d) a large hotel; (e) a first-run cinema; (f) a small café; (g) an ex-clusive restaurant; (h) an investment consultant; (i) city hall?

9. Which of the above businesses may be close to one another in the same part of downtown?

10. Could any of these activities also be found outside the downtown area of the city? Explain these cases.

Finally, a distinctive aspect of downtown is that for many citizens it sums up the character and status of the city, and for many visitors it makes the first im-pression and the lasting impact on the mind. When we think of Montreal we tend to think of Place Ville Marie and cosmopolitan downtown streets, not residential areas or industrial districts. Since there is some tendency to measure a town by the vitality and attractiveness of its downtown area, it is not surprising that in many cities local governments are actively and directly encouraging downtown redevelopment and improvement. In Halifax, for example, city officials and developers are co-operating closely to create the Scotia Square complex, shown in Figure 5-3, in the heart of downtown. Many Canadian cities used the 1967 Centennial Project opportunity to improve their central areas.

Fig. 5-3 Scotia Square, Halifax, under construction

And so, in most cities downtown is a vital and interesting place; in the words of the song:

> The lights are much brighter there,
> Forget all your troubles,
> Forget all your care.
> So go downtown,
> It will be great
> When you're downtown!

11. What does the writer of the song see as one function of downtown?
12. According to the song, what benefits can people enjoy by going downtown?
13. Do you think a successful downtown is necessary for a successful city?
14. What forces currently threaten the vitality of our downtown areas?

A few years ago it seemed that the combination of traffic congestion, the growth of competing suburban shopping centres, and the movement to suburban areas of some central activities such as wholesaling and manufacturing implied the imminent decay of the downtown area for many cities. Some observers suggested that in an automobile society a downtown was not necessary to a city, since people could easily travel to any location in the city for shopping or recreation or work and businesses could communicate with one another electronically, not needing to be clustered in one central place. It was argued that the dominance of downtown was only a phase in Canadian urban history, created by the technology of one form of transport, the streetcar, and destroyed by the technology of the automobile and electronic communications. The future shape of Canadian cities was predicted as something like Los Angeles, centreless and sprawling, "300 suburbs in search of a city." It is possible that this may still be the case. But from the present perspective it seems as though downtown is fighting back with vigour; merchants, developers and city officials are investing in the core areas of most Canadian cities. Even if downtown is no longer as important as it once was, it is by no means dying.

15. Using the street map of your own town or city, classify the land use of the downtown area. Several members of the class working co-operatively should be able to map the land use of the downtown area of even the larger cities.

16. Choose the busiest intersection of your town or city and walk out towards the fringe of the downtown area. Count the number of pedestrians you pass on each block and plot them on a graph like that shown below.

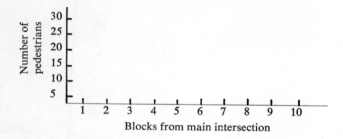

What conclusions can you draw about pedestrian traffic downtown and how do you account for it?

17. The class can be divided into pairs, each pair to take traffic counts at three times during the day (8:30 A.M., 12:00 noon and 5:00 P.M.) at selected points on the edge of the downtown area. The information can be arranged as follows and perhaps shown as flow lines (see page 57) on a map.

	Numbers					
	Inbound			Outbound		
	8:30	12:00	5:00	8:30	12:00	5:00
Cars						
Trucks						
Buses						
Other						

What conclusions might be drawn about the movement of traffic into the downtown area?

18. What evidence would suggest that the downtown area of your own town or city is either declining or growing in importance?

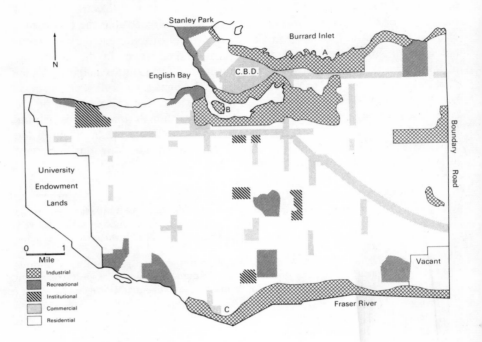

Fig. 5-4 Land use map of the City of Vancouver

3.   Industrial Areas

Most Canadian cities contain distinct industrial districts, which contain the industries forming part of the city's economic base or serving the city's own population.

19. How many different kinds of land use can you find marked on the map of Vancouver?
20. Identify the areas of industrial land use. Can you account for their location?
21. What kinds of industries might you expect to find in each of the various industrial districts? Why?
22. In which district might you expect to find: a sugar refinery, a boat repair yard, an oil refinery, a brewery, a small print shop, or a wholesale car distributor? Justify your choice in each case.
23. What specific advantages can you see in and around each industrial district which would help to support industry? Consider explicitly the areas marked A, B, and C.

Fig. 5-5 The Marpole industrial area in Vancouver

Many cities grew up from the start as industrial centres, like those specializing in mining or the processing of raw materials. Other cities soon developed industries along with their original founding functions as, for example, those ports or transport centres which now also process goods in shipment, or repair transport equipment. Nowadays, within most modern cities there are usually several industrial districts, and the various recognizable districts contain typical kinds of manufacturing plants. The types of industries in each district depend on the particular advantages that the particular industrial area offers, and the particular location needs of different kinds of industrial plant.

For example, most Canadian cities have an old established industrial district near the centre of town, which is often still the most important industrial area. In coastal and lakeside cities it is invariably a waterfront location, a point where all the transportation systems come together (road, rail, water), and the collection of materials and distribution of manufactured goods is relatively simple. In inland cities, a riverside location is common; this sometimes is a site that offers power, or water supply advantages, as well as transport convenience.

24. What industries can you identify in Figure 5-5?
25. How would you explain the preponderance of forest products industries in this location?
26. Explain the presence of log booms and of scows.
27. Refer to the map shown in Figure 5-4. Why might the Marpole area have been an attractive location for some of Vancouver's earlier industries?

What advantages does it retain at the present time? (This area is marked
C in Figure 5-4.)

28. From what places do the industries in the photograph probably draw their
material inputs, and to what places may they send their products?

Typically, such older, waterfront industrial districts now include food processing industries (sugar mills, flour mills), non-metallic mineral industries (cement
works), forest products industries, metal industries, and transport equipment
repair industries. These tend to be heavier industries, using large amounts of
material inputs. They usually look beyond the city for these inputs and usually
sell their products outside the city also. Thus they are "externally oriented"
industries, and they choose a site with good access to these external suppliers
and markets.

The core area itself (usually the downtown "fringe," the zone around the
central business district itself) often contains some distinctive industries, usually
smaller-scale activities employing few workers, or perhaps firms crowding
machinery and workers into multi-storey factories on the expensive central sites.
Typical central area industrial activities include printing, publishing, clothing
manufacturing, the manufacture of jewellery or specialized machinery. These
activities tend to serve the city itself rather than external markets and can be
called "internally oriented" activities. A central location is convenient to serve
this urban market and also gives access to the sort of labour often needed by
these firms. Downtown also supplies the small, adaptable work spaces these
businesses tend to need, in the form of lofts, converted warehouses, or old residences.

Over the last few decades, zoning ordinances have acted to confine industrial activities to a few types of location within Canadian cities; for example, to
railway-side and *highway-side* industrial districts. The latter usually contain the

George Allen Aerial Photos Ltd.

Fig. 5-6 A modern industrial district, Lake City Industrial Park, Vancouver, B.C.

newer activities which have developed after 1945, and the lighter industries, as well as wholesalers and service activities. Access to labour, to materials, and to external and internal markets *via* the freeway system, plus the possibility of finding large sites convenient for the layout of the plant, for employee parking, and for future expansion, are some of the factors behind the recent growth of these suburban highway-side industrial districts. Some of the most recent of these are carefully planned *industrial parks,* where a single developer lays out a site and builds factories for a number of firms.

29. Can you identify any industries in Figure 5-6?
30. How does the appearance of the industrial area in Figure 5-6 compare to that in Figure 5-5? What considerations might be behind the more spacious layout of plants in Figure 5-6?
31. Figure 5-7 includes names of industries located in this industrial park. What characteristics do these industries have in common?
32. What facilities do the developers stress in advertising for tenants? What might some of the advantages and disadvantages of locating in such a site be for some firms?

Fig. 5-7 An advertisement for Lake City Industrial Park

Greater Vancouver, British Columbia

Good Neighbours Make the Difference... At Lake City Industrial Park in B.C.

Already, some of Canada's foremost companies have firmly established themselves in the West's finest located and most prestigious industrial park – Lake City!

Set in the geographical heart of Greater Vancouver, Lake City has everything going for it . . . level terrain, excellent footings, good elevation, and full access to highway, railway and sea-way. Maximum services are provided and a variety of purchase and lease plans are available.

If you are looking West – and beyond – see Lake City first.

Some industries may locate not in distinct districts but rather alone or in isolated sites in cities; these include the noxious or dangerous industries, such as oil refineries, fish canneries, and pulp mills.

As mentioned, a recent trend has been to try to segregate industrial land uses from other land uses in cities, and to improve the appearance of industrial districts. Old industrial areas were not renowned for their neatness or beauty. Economic efficiency was (and still is) the main criterion of location and operation for most urban industries. In the search for economic efficiency, factors of appearance of the plant or its effect on the environment were usually ignored. Many established industrial districts continue to pollute the areas around them with their waste products, noises, smell, and appearance. We tended to tolerate this in the past, thankful for the jobs and prosperity brought to the city by industry, and not counting the *social costs* of the polluted air and water, blighted residential districts, congestion, and health hazards borne by the city at large. Now we are trying to avoid these costs that arise out of the mislocation and poor operation of urban industries. Thus we now see the development of industrial parks in suburban areas, the decentralization of industry from central locations, and also the redevelopment of old industrial slums like Vancouver's False Creek area and Toronto's waterfront, as well as a general tightening of pollution and zoning laws in many cities.

33. Refer to Figures 5-5 and 5-6. What evidence of industrial pollution can you see in the photographs? Who would be affected by it? What immediate solutions can you suggest for the specific kinds of pollution visible? What difficulties would stand in the way of implementing these solutions?

34. From what has been said in the text, where in the city might you expect to find:
    a) a modern light industrial plant producing for the local market?
    b) a small factory needing a lot of unskilled labour?
    c) an older, heavy industrial plant sending most of its output outside the city?
    d) a large plant needing a great deal of space for storage of bulky materials?
    e) a small, highly automated factory assembling light components into goods for a local market?

4.   Commercial Activities

Commercial activities such as stores, personal service establishments (barbers, beauty shops), repair shops and so on have distinct patterns of location within North American cities. Some geographers argue that if we look carefully at the location of such businesses, then in most cities we can detect *business centres, business ribbons,* and *specialized business districts.*

The business *centres* range from small neighbourhood centres to the downtown shopping district itself, with a range of other business centres in between. In a large city, one may detect "community centres" and "regional centres," and perhaps also an intermediate "shopping goods centre" between the community and regional centres. The important point is that each of these shopping centres has a typical number and range of stores within it. For example, in large American cities like Chicago an arrangement of centres like that summarized in Table 5-1 has been described.

35. Can you identify the equivalent of these centres in your own town or city? Can you account for any differences in your local area?
36. From what kind of trade area may each of the above types of centre draw its customers? (Refer to Part Four.)
37. What business centre stands above the regional centres in the city? What kinds of goods and services might it provide?

Smaller stores may exist outside such centres, to cater to late-night or weekend demands, but may find it increasingly hard to compete against the neighbourhood concentrations, especially as more and more people shop by automobile.

These business centres are often called a *business hierarchy*. This somewhat resembles a broad-based pyramid of centres. At the bottom is a large number of the small neighbourhood centres, with rather restricted trade areas and thus closely spaced over the urban landscape. These are packed or contained within the trade areas of the fewer, larger, more widely spaced community centres that stand above them in the hierarchy. The upper levels of the hierarchy are made up of even fewer regional centres spaced farther apart in the city. At the top of the pyramid is the unique downtown shopping district, usually the only centre with a city-wide trade area. The basis of this hierarchy, as discussed in Part Four, is the fact that different kinds of stores have different threshold populations; thus the stores with large threshold populations are few in number, and

Table 5-1   Urban Business Centres in Chicago

Type of Centre	Number of Businesses	Types of Businesses	Examples of Businesses
Neighbourhood	40	25	Grocery stores, supermarket, café, bank, barber.
Community	70-80	35	As above, plus hardware, shoe stores, real estate and doctors' offices.
Shopping goods	150	50	As above, plus children's wear, flower stores, cinema, dentists.
Regional centres	200	70	As above, plus small department stores, camera stores, medical and dental services.

SOURCE: Brian Berry, *Commercial Structure and Commercial Blight* (Chicago: University of Chicago Press, 1963).

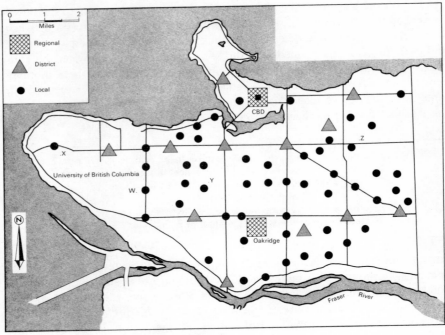

Fig. 5-8 The business hierarchy in Vancouver

are strategically located in the city so as to be conveniently accessible to larger numbers of people.

38. Figure 5-8 represents the business hierarchy in Vancouver; here the hierarchy is best described in three layers (excluding the central business district — the CBD) instead of four as in Chicago, and here they are called local (neighbourhood), district (community-shopping goods), and regional centres. How many centres are there at each level in the hierarchy? Explain the greater density of local centres in the inner parts of the city. Measure the distances between some of the local centres, and also the separation between the district centres; explain the differences in distance. How are the district centres located with respect to major urban streets?

39. In which centres would households located at W, X, Y, and Z probably shop for: (a) groceries; (b) inexpensive clothes; (c) children's clothes; (d) expensive clothes and gifts? Link these households to the centres you choose by flow lines. What does this tell us about the trade areas of the centres at different levels of the hierarchy?

Of course, different centres in the same level of the hierarchy do not always contain exactly the same numbers and types of store. Neighbourhood centres in poorer parts of town, where purchasing power is low and tastes are different, will contain fewer stores, and fewer of the more specialized store types (gift stores or boutiques), but may have more second-hand stores. In fact, the whole business hierarchy may be less well developed and less elaborate over the poorer areas of town. In areas of town with a particular ethnic or demographic bias,

Fig. 5-9 A planned shopping centre, Oakridge, in Vancouver

stores in the business centres reflect this also. For example, on Vancouver's Commercial Drive, the goods in the grocery stores reflect the concentrations of Italians nearby; on Broadway the cafés, supermarkets, and bakeries have a Greek flavour; and on Oak Street, the delicatessens reflect the local concentration of Jewish population. In suburban Richmond, a community-level centre probably has garden shops, handyman stores, and children's wear stores, reflecting the particular preoccupation and needs of suburbanites.

40. If you live in a city, identify two or three "neighbourhood centres" of about equal rank in the business hierarchy. What kind of stores are common to them all? What stores are found only in one centre, and not in the others? Explain these exceptions.

A new feature of many large cities is that *planned shopping centres* are being established to rival the old, established centres that grew up around former streetcar stops or at major street intersections. The planned centres (i.e., uniformly designed stores on a large site owned by one company) usually operate at the community or regional level, and often contain a branch department store, a large supermarket, and several specialty stores.

41. About what "level" in the business hierarchy is the centre in Figure 5-9? About how many stores and stores of what type might you expect

to find there? Does it seem to be a successful centre?

42. From the photograph, what factors seem to have been considered in choosing a site for this shopping centre? (Consider especially the location of the centre relative to downtown; location relative to major highways; nature of the surrounding residential area in terms of density of population and its social character.)

43. From the evidence of the photograph, what advantages to shoppers do planned centres seem to offer? What advantages to merchants?

44. What effect does the opening of a planned centre in a location have on other unplanned centres nearby? Can you identify any centres which may be affected by the large planned centre in the photograph? (Refer to Figure 5-8.)

45. Are there any planned shopping centres in your town? When were they built? Visit one and identify the stores it contains. What might be the impact of this centre on nearby unplanned centres? How could you design a study to measure the actual impact of the centre? Carry out the study and discuss the results.

Business *ribbons* are common in Canadian cities. These are the strips of stores and service businesses that line the major highways on the outskirts and towards the centre of the larger cities. The business types are those that cater to the needs of the passing highway population itself, rather than the residential population of the area behind the highway. Figure 5-10 shows clearly how these business ribbons develop along the major highways and crosstown highways of the city, especially the inner city where approach traffic is heavy. For example,

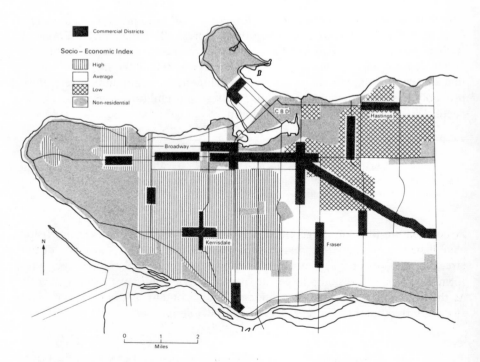

Fig. 5-10 Urban arterial commercial districts in the City of Vancouver

on the edge of town, ribbon businesses include hotels, motels, restaurants, and so on, while closer to the city centre they include drive-in cafés, car washes, and repair shops. Another type of business often found in a ribbon location may not appeal to passing motorists but may be a business which needs large amounts of space and is unable to pay the high rent of a shopping centre for their larger sites. Examples are lumber yards, discount stores, carpet stores, funeral parlors, and auction rooms.

Frequently, business centres and business ribbons are hard to tell apart in large cities; major thoroughfares are almost continuously lined with businesses in an apparently confused fashion. However, closer examination often reveals regularly spaced *nucleations* or thickenings of residentially-oriented convenience-goods and shopping-goods stores along such streets, with more varied highway-oriented businesses strung out at lower densities between them. In even the seemingly most confused urban land use situations, elements of orderly patterns can usually be detected with close observation.

Specialized districts are found in many medium and large cities. These districts may be in part of a large business centre (for example, the specialized ladies' wear district of the downtown area, or the men's wear district often found adjacent to the financial district of the downtown area), or in a specialized strip of a business ribbon (for example, a furniture district or an automobile row, like Vancouver's Broadway, or Toronto's Danforth Avenue).

46. How many establishments of the same kind can you detect in the photograph? Why do you think these businesses cluster together in this fashion and in this location?
47. What other type of business shows similar tendencies to cluster? Which businesses are never clustered together? Explain these latter cases.

Fig. 5-11 An automobile row

Clustering allows stores to attract more customers, since customers can compare items and prices on a single trip or combine purchases of similar goods on a single trip. It is also convenient for merchants in that service businesses may spring up nearby to serve the cluster (dressmakers will situate in the vicinity of ladies' wear districts, for example). And once a specialized shopping district becomes "known" it will acquire a kind of prestige and attract other stores of the same kind to itself, reinforcing its own attraction.

48. Where would you expect to find in the city businesses of the following type, and why: (a) a branch department store; (b) a "ma and pa" grocery store; (c) an exclusive dress shop; (d) a builder's yard; (e) a medical specialist; (f) a European bakery; (g) a variety store? Which of these businesses are you unlikely to find in the same business centre, and why?

5.   Forces Affecting Urban Land Use

Urban land use patterns are quite intelligible if they are looked at carefully. Land is not used in an accidental fashion in cities, activities do not locate at whim. An important factor in sorting activities and their typical locations in cities is economic *competition,* that is, the contest by particular kinds of activities for the sites in the city that best suit their own needs. Where several kinds of activity desire the same site, it usually goes to the user who can earn most from it, and thus afford to pay more for it as rent. In this way, the most desirable central sites are captured by the high earning commercial functions, and central sites come to have a high value as they are heavily competed for. Industries bid against other users for highway-side and riverside sites and preempt these. Most residential activities (discussed in more detail in Part Six) are poor competitors for land, unless they are of the multi-storey type, and fit between the strategic spaces occupied by commercial and industrial uses. Even so the more affluent residents still claim the more desirable residential sites, and occupy larger lots at lower densities.

This process of competition normally works within a land-use framework established early in the life of any city. The detailed topography of the site usually influences the location of the first activities which are the functional nucleus of the city. Main roads, public transport routes and railway lines, and major institutional land uses (city hall, law courts, and so on) are usually located next. Competition for spaces then positions the activities and population of the growing city within the framework established by these *dominant land uses* which become the reference points for the growth of the city.

Of course the process of land-use competition is not completely smooth. Nowadays it is partly controlled by zoning laws and public planning, which suspend the process of competition if it seems likely to produce a city plan incompatible with public social goals. Thus zoning prevents commercial districts encroaching on nearby residential districts, or prevents single-family residential areas of the inner city from turning into apartment districts under the pressure of demand for urban living space. Public regulations maintain open spaces and parks in valuable central areas. Sometimes even without regulation, the economic pressures of competition fail to bring about apparently logical land use changes, due to the influence of non-economic factors. For example, an upper class residential area, or an ethnic residential area in a central location, may not be taken over by higher-rent-paying commercial functions because the people refuse to vacate an area that has a sentimental value for them.

49. Identify the major areas of public open space (parks, squares, etc.) in your city. When were they established? How have they affected the use of land in the adjacent areas? Suppose these parks were turned over to private development; what kind of land uses would develop on them, and why?
50. Obtain a zoning map from the public library or city hall of your town. Look at it carefully. What kinds of land uses are described by the zoning laws? What seem to be the principles of zoning? Have any changes in local zoning been made recently in your city? With what effects? Do you think that the form of your city would be very different if there were no zoning rules at all?

SIX

Man in the City

1. Introduction

In this section, though interest in the internal organization of the modern Canadian city is maintained, concentration is on the distribution of people within the city rather than on activities. The character of the urban population and the nature of residential areas will be discussed in some detail, together with some of the patterns of movements of the urban population. How can we best describe the highly varied populations of our cities? How can we explain the contrasts in the character of various residential areas, for example, the contrast between the "two sides of the tracks" that exist in all Canadian cities? How and why do areas change their character over time? What kinds of flows of people tie one part of the city to another? These are some of the important questions considered in this section.

The most important single use of land in cities is for residential purposes. Cities are founded for economic or political purposes, and grow as they enlarge or add to their economic functions. But after that, the city is a collection of people who work in or serve these founding economic activities. Much of the urban space is given over to housing these people. Thus the impression we get of a large city from the air or from a high vantage point is, above all, of a sea of residences – houses, yards, apartment buildings, and so on.

Many of the examples and exercises which follow deal with Vancouver, B.C. This is partly because this is the city the authors know best. But also it is the result of a decision to concentrate on one city in particular, so that the various exercises have a cumulative effect. As you do the exercises you should be building up a large amount of information and impressions about Canada's third largest city; and especially about its social geography. In addition, it will be an advantage to use the various photographs, maps, and tables of this part of the book when you are attempting any particular exercise. Of course, the conclusions arrived at in this section will be generalizations, applicable to other Canadian cities. Therefore, you should try to think of the relevance of the conclusions you come to in the exercises for your own city. (An interesting exercise would be to try to gather together material for your own city similar to what is gathered here for Vancouver, to replicate the exercises and compare your conclusions.)

2.   The Residents

Residential areas within the city are markedly different one from another. The city population itself is highly varied and different kinds of people tend to live in different parts of the city. In fact geographers and sociologists suggest that urban populations vary in three basic ways: in terms of *social class, demographic aspects,* and *ethnic origins.* These different types of urban dwellers have different residential needs and patterns of location.

Consider first the matter of *social class.* The differences in social class between groups are complex but are based on differences in income, education, and occupation, and are reflected in such things as accent, patterns of consumption, social behaviour, and political attitudes. These circumstances create a range of status groups, from the wealthy, old, established families of eastern Canada at the "top" to the skid road derelicts at the "bottom"; we describe the gradations in between in several terms: "upper," "middle," and "lower" classes, "white collar" and "blue collar," and so on. In Canada, a degree of mobility between classes is possible; a person can be born in one class and move "up" to another class by education, hard work, or marriage.

Most important for our purposes is that the different social groups do tend to occupy different parts of the city. The urban area thus becomes differentiated into *social areas* occupied by different socio-economic groups. To put it another way, a *physical distance* as well as a *social distance* develops between social groups in the city. Shaughnessy Heights and East Hastings Street in Vancouver are about six miles apart physically, but are totally different social worlds.

The higher socio-economic groups tend to occupy certain kinds of areas in Canadian cities. They avoid sites close to incompatible land uses (noisy factories, busy highways), and seek sites with convenient access to downtown facilities but also with qualities of quietness, privacy, aspect, and view. Elevated slopes or lakesides or riversides are often preferred, like Montreal's Westmount, Vancouver's Shaughnessy Heights, and Calgary's Mount Royal. The poorer, lower socio-economic groups, less able to afford to compete for residential sites, must occupy the areas left free by the more competitive land users. Their residences thus crowd onto smaller lots, in sites adjacent to industrial or commercial land uses, sometimes on poorly drained, low-lying land, without prospect or view.

As the city grows, the location of the later developing residential areas of the various social types is influenced by the location of existing social areas. Upper social areas tend to develop adjacent to the existing upper status areas, so that *wedges* or *sectors* of upper status areas can be found in many Canadian cities, radiating from an original nucleus of high status housing. Lower status groups occupy complementary sectors in other parts of the city. For example, in nineteenth century Vancouver, a contrast early developed between the upper class West End, close to the beach and park, and the lower class East End area, behind the waterfront industrial district. As Vancouver expanded, higher class groups consistently located on the western side of the city, in the "shadow" of the original élite area and discreetly removed from the rough and tumble eastern

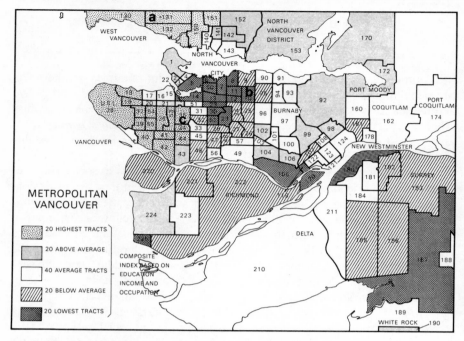

Fig. 6-1 Socio-economic areas of metropolitan Vancouver

1. Identify the high and low socio-economic areas on the map. What kind of people (in terms of social class) probably live in these various areas?
2. Plot the highest and lowest areas on a separate map. Can you explain the location of these areas?
3. Make a list of the advantages and disadvantages of living in the areas marked A and B on the map, under the following headings: (a) nearness to downtown, (b) nearness to industrial areas, (c) view, (d) crowding, (e) access to open space, (f) elevation, (g) proximity to highways. (You may find it helpful to refer to Figure 5-4.)

part of the city, which grew by the attraction of its own compatible population. In this way, early contrasts in urban land use are built into the organization of the later city.

Urban residential areas may not retain one distinctive social character. Over time, a once fashionable upper class area may gradually change into a congested slum or a student apartment district; a row of rundown nineteenth century houses may be discovered by the middle class and restored to elegance. As the different social groups of the city grow, they may grow out of their established districts and invade neighbouring areas, perhaps occupied by other social groups; the invasion may eventually result in the virtually complete replacement of one group by another in the area, i.e., the *succession* of the invading group.

Fig. 6-2 Sequence of development in Vancouver's West End

The West End is marked with an A in Fig. 6-3.

Residential History

1. Period of single family residences 1889-1910.
a) 1889-99. Development as elite residential area.
b) 1900-10. Addition of middle income population.

2. Period of conversion to multiple family use 1910-1955.
a) 1910-26. Sporadic conversions, and growth of commercial functions in some areas.
b) 1927-40. Regular conversion of older homes to multi-family use.
c) 1940-55. Rapid conversion of remaining dwellings plus apartment building.

3. Growth of apartment buildings 1955—Rapid growth of new apartment buildings, especially after 1961.

4. What kind of people probably occupied this area during each of these periods?
5. What attractions did each group find in the area at each period?
6. What factors helped the transferral of the area from one group to another? Why did the transitions probably occur at the times that they did?
7. What evidence of these various phases can you see in the photograph of the present landscape of the West End?

Succession in an area may occur quite rapidly if the invading group is ethnically as well as socially different from the original group. The original inhabitants may speedily evacuate the area if they feel the newcomers will change its character. For example, negro ghettoes tend to expand by invasion into neighbouring low income white areas, in a process which is slow at first, as one or two negro families "bust the block" against resistance, then speeds up when most white families evacuate the changing area.

Canadian urban populations are different in *demographic* terms as well as social class terms. Age and sex differences are related to the *life cycle* of the urban population. Thus one could say that the typical Canadian urban household consists of two parents and two or three children (where the size of the family is often related to social class). However, this unit is a temporary condition for most of its members. Children grow up, and leave the family unit to set up independent households as students or young workers. They may then

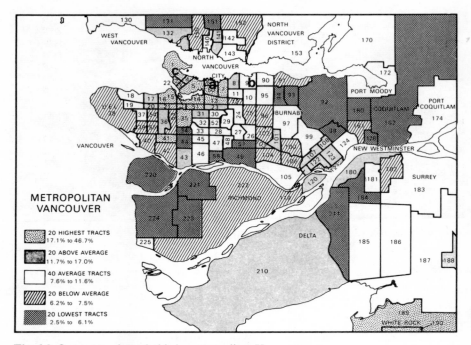

Fig. 6-3 One-person households in metropolitan Vancouver

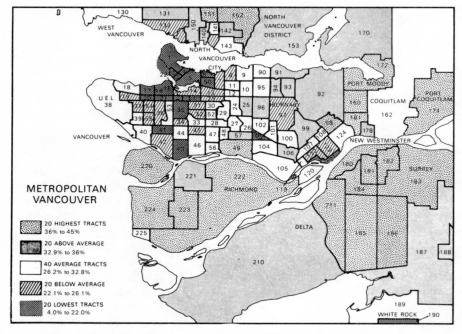

Fig. 6-4 Percentage of population 0-14 years of age in metropolitan Vancouver

live alone or share an apartment with room-mates. Young adults marry, and while childless, may continue to live in rooms or an apartment as a "two-person household"; older people whose children have grown up also constitute two-person households. In all large cities there also exist "single-person households" of the widowed, divorced, or unmarried adults. Less commonly nowadays there may be large households of "extended families," of adults, children, grandparents, and even other relatives (sons-in-law, etc.) living under the same roof; this is more typical of the poor, or of rural migrant families.

These different household types tend to have different residential needs, and to locate in certain parts of the city, so that various parts of the city come to be demographically distinct from one another as well as socially distinct.

8. What kinds of families probably live in the differently shaded areas on Figure 6-3? What will probably be the relative ratios of old to young and men to women in the areas marked A and B on the map? Justify your answers. (The area marked A is shown in Figure 6-2 and that marked B in Figure 4-4.)
9. On a separate map plot the areas with the higher and lowest proportions of one-person households. Why should these areas have such concentrations of these types of households? (Look carefully at the key to this map before attempting an answer. Why could the map be misleading?)
10. What kinds of families live in the differently shaded areas on Figure 6-4?
11. Explain the concentration of children in the outer urban areas.

In general, the "typical" family household described earlier tends to occupy the broad outer zone of single family dwellings that surrounds the central core of the city. The more distant and more recent suburbs of the city edge tend to be inhabited by new families with younger children, so it is here that the proportion of dependent children in the population is higher than in any other part of the city. These families are seeking space to bring up a growing family, and the suburbs are the only place to provide it at a reasonable price. They may also be seeking relief from urban congestion and pollution, plus proximity to the countryside and neighbourliness, when they move to the suburbs at this important phase of the life cycle.

The households without children, until recently at least, tended to occupy an inner zone close to the centre of the city. Here, large old houses, no longer suitable for single family use, could be converted into rooming houses for single people, or to apartments for young couples. Such households do not demand the space and privacy of the child-centred family, and appreciate an inner city location for its proximity to downtown workplaces and to recreational and entertainment facilities. The better-off among these childless households (professional groups, young marrieds with combined incomes, and older couples returning from the suburbs after children have left home) tend to occupy the new, elegant apartments of the inner city apartment districts. Most large Canadian cities have, in fact, recently gone through an inner city apartment construction spurt, as the post-war "baby boom" comes of age in conditions of affluence.

The demographic profile of different areas of the city can be very distinctive, as the data below show.

Table 6-1   Vancouver: Population of Selected Census Tracts, 1966

	TRACT A			TRACT B	
Age	Males	Females	Age	Males	Females
0-4	160	126	0-4	559	536
5-9	81	90	5-9	637	646
10-14	86	80	10-14	407	426
15-19	141	217	15-19	234	234
20-24	674	914	20-24	132	156
25-34	1,200	969	25-34	572	672
35-44	654	596	35-44	636	593
45-54	522	769	45-54	298	230
55-64	520	729	55-64	70	63
65-69	225	343	65-69	11	36
70+	654	1,023	70+	41	59
	4,917	5,856		3,597	3,651

SOURCE: Dominion Bureau of Statistics, *Census of Canada,* 1966.

12. Construct an age-sex pyramid from the data in Table 6-1 for each of the census areas. What do the pyramids show? Is this picture consistent with the information in Figures 6-3 and 6-4? (Tracts A and B are areas A and B in Figure 6-1.)
13. What other parts of the city may show similar age-sex profiles to the ones illustrated? Explain this.
14. What might be some of the social problems, and the problems of supply of public services, to areas like the ones for which data are given? How can these problems be overcome?

A recent trend is the growth of apartment districts in non-central locations in Canadian cities, in areas like Vancouver's Kerrisdale or Toronto's Don Mills. This tends to break down the demographic monotony of the suburban areas. Such suburban apartment districts tend to gather together older individuals, or couples whose children have grown up, and who want to give up a large suburban family home. They may also contain younger people who commute to non-central workplaces.

Ethnic differences among the Canadian urban population arise from the fact that Canada is essentially a community of immigrants. Some Canadian cities may have an ethnically homogeneous population; for example, many of the smaller towns of Ontario and Nova Scotia, such as Peterborough, Saint John, and Sydney, may list over two-thirds of their population as native-born Canadians of Anglo-Saxon stock; small towns in southern Quebec such as Trois Rivières and Shawinigan may be over ninety per cent French descent. But many Canadian cities, and all the larger ones, have significant ethnic minorities of new immigrants from continental Europe, Asia, or the United States, and certainly they have many first generation Canadians, born of immigrant parents.

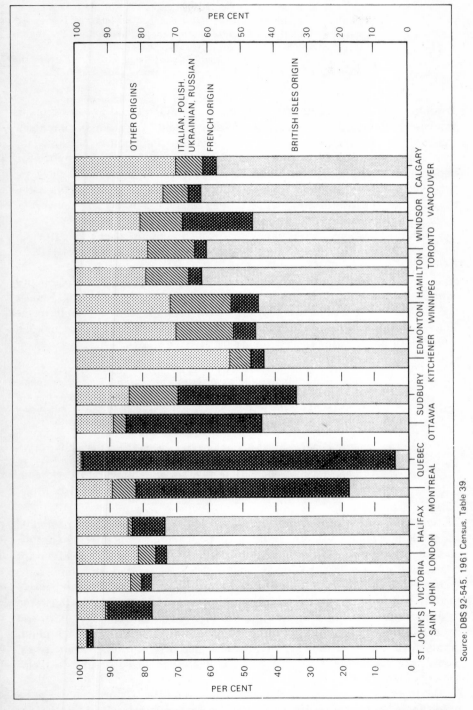

Fig. 6-5 Distribution of population among four ethnic origin categories in metropolitan areas of Canada

15. Arrange the cities in Figure 6-5 in order, according to the percentage of population of British Isles origin. How can you explain the differences? How can you explain the particular ethnic composition of St. John's, Quebec, Sudbury, Kitchener, Winnipeg, and Calgary?
16. What factors attract new immigrants to particular cities? What are the problems faced by a city with a large immigrant population?

Toronto with its large population of recent Italian, Greek and Portugese immigrants, the Prairie towns with East European and American communities, Vancouver with its Dutch, German, and Chinese communities, are only the most obvious examples. The larger cities tend to attract immigrants by the job opportunities they offer, and because they are also often ports of entry for newcomers. Particular ethnic groups tend to accumulate in particular cities because the exchange of information among migrants attracts later movers to the same destinations as earlier ones from the same origins.

Within a city, immigrant ethnic groups also tend to cluster in particular locations. Toronto's "Little Italy" districts, Vancouver's Commercial Drive Italian district or its East End Chinatown, are clear examples, because the ethnic groups involved are large and visible, and have developed a distinctive *cultural landscape* in their part of the city, in the store fronts, cafés, house decoration, and street life that they create. Figure 6-6 shows this well; in the Toronto example it is clear that the district has not always been Italian and that a process of invasion and succession has occurred.

17. Identify areas in Figure 6-7 with the largest proportion of immigrant population. How can you explain the location of these areas? The areas marked A, B, and C in Figure 6-7 are areas of concentration of Asian, Italian, and West European immigrants respectively. How can you explain these particular locations?
18. Compare Figure 6-7 with Figures 6-1, 6-3 and 6-4. What might the demographic and social characteristics of the immigrant population be?
19. What are the advantages and disadvantages of having some physical separation of different ethnic groups in the city?

These ethnic areas exist in part because particular ethnic groups have limited economic prospects and must locate in parts of the city where rents are low, and where workplaces are near. Inner city immigrant districts have existed for a long time in larger eastern Canadian cities; they developed as poor immigrants (at first Irish and Polish, later Italian and Greek) sought out the cheap housing the city had to offer. Once established, though, these immigrant districts tend to attract new immigrants by seeming to offer companionship and old world culture in the new land. By a process of invasion and succession, such immigrants might expand into neighbouring areas, and drive out other ethnic types. Thus, once established by circumstance ethnic areas tend to reinforce themselves by choice.

This *spatial segregation* of ethnic groups into local areas of the city can be unfortunate if it tends to perpetuate ethnic prejudices in the society, or if it leads to a ghetto mentality in immigrants, but it can be beneficial also if it helps the

Fig. 6-6 Left: Vancouver's Chinatown. Right: Toronto's "Little Italy"

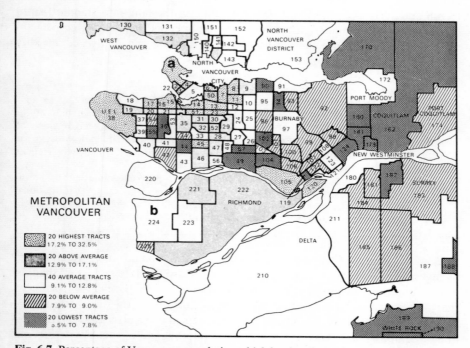

Fig. 6-7 Percentage of Vancouver population which has immigrated to the city, 1946-1961

adjustment of immigrants to the new culture, and if it minimizes (*via* separation) conflict between groups. At least in Canada the segregation is not imposed by law, and Canadian institutions and practices encourage the assimilation of all groups into one of the two mainstreams of Canadian culture, while also respecting a variety of cultural expressions.

The distinctiveness of a residential area of the city then may be due to the distinctiveness of urban residents in social class, demographic or ethnic terms. These factors are not independent, and when overlaid and combined in various ways, create a rich variety of population groups and associated residential areas within the city, whose location and function can be interpreted in the ways suggested here.

3.   Residential Areas: The Residences

Urban residential areas can be looked at in terms of residences as well as residents, that is, in terms of the *morphology* of the area, or its appearance due to the pattern of streets, the number and spacing of houses, the architecture of houses and the layout of gardens.

In most Canadian cities the predominant pattern in the layout of residential areas is the grid-iron pattern: a rectangular block of standard size, subdivided into housing lots of standard size, often 60′ x 120′. This reflects the circumstances of land surveying, subdivision, and land marketing in the nineteenth and early twentieth centuries. Parcelling of the land into standard sized lots, irrespective of underlying topography or intended use, was a convenient way of getting land into the market when land was a speculative commodity and cities were growing rapidly.

20. On Figure 6-8, one inch represents about 600 feet. What is the size of a typical city block in the residential area in the upper right half of the photograph? About how many houses are there per block? How does the density of population here compare with the area of boulevards in the upper centre of the picture? (This is Vancouver's Shaughnessy Heights area, marked with a C in Figure 6-1).

21. On the photograph, identify areas of (a) upper class housing, (b) lower class housing, (c) apartments, (d) commercial land uses, (e) institutional uses, (f) recreational open space. What difficulties does a grid-iron street plan seem to create for these various urban land uses?

Occasionally in the older part of town this rigid street plan is interrupted by the avenues and boulevards of an upper class residential estate, e.g., the Shaughnessy Heights development in Vancouver. And of course the post-war suburbs that ring all cities have tried to break away from the grid-iron pattern; developers now buy tracts of land and lay out streets in more elaborate geometrics, in an attempt to segregate traffic, reduce monotony, and attract higher income buyers.

Lockwood Survey Corp. Ltd.

Fig. 6-8 Aerial view of a typical residential area, showing the street pattern

Fig. 6-9 Variations in residences

22. In Figure 6-9, which of the photographs are of "upper" and "lower" social status areas, and which of older and newer areas? What details of the appearance of the areas help you make up your mind in each case?

The appearance of houses in the various residential areas of the city is related to, among other things, the *social status* of inhabitants and the *age* of the house. Social status is related to the ability to buy, maintain, and embellish a large house, and so in the upper class sectors houses are large, well spaced, well maintained, and have well-kept grounds. Houses are also *social symbols,* so the details of the house design (windows, entrance, garages) are reflections of the inhabitant's aspirations and life styles. Thus, upper class groups tend to stress things like privacy, exclusiveness, and leisure in their life styles, and the appearance of upper class residential areas reflects this, in the shaded lots, imposing entrances to houses, many-roomed houses for internal privacy, provision of leisure equipment such as pools and tennis courts, and so on. Upper class residential sectors also show the greatest variety of architectural house styles, since this group tends to experiment with novelty in design. Some successful styles then are imitated by lower social groups at later dates. This process tends to create more monotonous residential landscapes in middle and lower class areas. The most monotonous landscapes of all are the recent lower-middle-class suburbs, easy-to-build variations on the few fashionable styles of the last three decades.

Age is related to appearance in housing, since the older houses obviously must reflect the styles, technology, and needs of the period in which they were built. Within the city a gradient exists from the older (large, high, brick) central city houses to the newest (low, wood, and glass) houses and garages on the still growing edge of the city. In the centre of the largest cities, however, where the oldest houses are becoming obsolete, their old form unsuitable for contemporary functions, and expensive to maintain and repair, there may be a process of replacement by new residences (apartments or town houses). Only a few houses survive to cross the threshold into the "ancient monument" class where their very age protects them from destruction. In the centre of the city there is the greatest variety of residential types, the greatest mixture of houses in terms of age, social character, and style.

4.   The Mobility of Urban Residents

The city population is very mobile; urbanites change their residences several times in their lives and urban areas change in character over a period of time. In fact, in any single year, about 20 per cent of the households of a large city may change residence. Our modern urban society is clearly a highly mobile one. In this section, then, we look more closely at this question of *intra-urban residential mobility* and try to discover what kind of people move most frequently in the city, why they move, and how they go about moving.

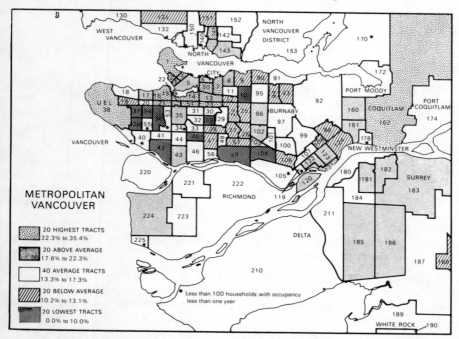

Fig. 6-10 Residential mobility in Vancouver: percentage of households with occupancy of less than 1 year

23. In Figure 6-10 identify the districts where a relatively large proportion of the population has moved into the area within the previous twelve months, and areas where the residential population is more stable. What kind of people probably live in these different areas? (Refer to Figures 6-1, 6-3 and 6-4).

24. Which particular areas of the city have a higher population turnover than others? Why should these areas attract the more mobile population, and thus be "residentially unstable" areas?

It is clear from Figure 6-10 that again there are systematic differences among various residential areas in the city, this time in terms of the proportion of recent residents in the local population. In some areas, people are always moving in and out, and these are residentially unstable areas, with few long term residents. University areas, apartment districts, and inner city residential areas are such cases, since these are populated by mobile groups such as students, young unmarried workers, or immigrants. Middle income suburbs of the outer city have a higher degree of stability, since the population is tied down by the needs of raising children and by financial limits on moving at this period of pressure on the family budget. Thus, an inner-outer city contrast exists here, as with other aspects of the urban population.

Figure 6-10 hints at and Table 6-2 confirms that different urban types have different propensities to change residence within the city.

Table 6-2   Percentage of Males Moving Annually Within the American City

Education (yrs.)	18-24	24-34	Age 35-44	45-64	65+
0-8	—	24.1	14.2	8.5	6.6
9-11	—	26.2	10.7	7.8	5.2
12	—	18.9	11.1	7.0	5.4
13+	—	19.4	10.3	7.5	5.9
Occupation					
White Collar	27.2	19.9	9.4	6.3	3.0
Manual	30.4	22.9	12.1	8.2	5.9
Service	25.6	25.5	16.7	9.0	5.9
Farm	15.9	11.1	9.5	6.8	2.0

SOURCE: J. Simmons, "Changing Residences in the City: A Review of Intra-Urban Mobility," *Geographical Review* (October, 1968), p. 625.

25. Using Table 6-2, what is the relationship between age and the propensity to move within the city? Why should this be so? Which age group has the greatest propensity to move?

26. Is there any relation between education and tendency to move?

27. What is the relationship between occupational types and tendency to move? Which occupational groups are the most likely to move, and the least likely to move? How might this be explained?

28. Would you expect the following groups to be (a) very mobile, (b) somewhat mobile, (c) not very mobile?
    1. Older business man.

2. Young well-educated executive.
3. Older farm worker.
4. Young labourer, no high school education.
5. Middle aged mechanic, no high school education.

What other information would help you to judge the relative mobility of the above types?

What is the reason for these numerous changes of residence by city dwellers over the years, especially by the younger, less well educated and lower social groups? Actually the reasons are as numerous as the moves, but many of them may be summarized as three basic types, namely changes in *household circumstances,* related to the life cycle discussed earlier; changes in *household finances,* making a move necessary or possible for a family; or changes in the *nature of the residential area* itself, pushing the family away from the old home.

Consider the following imaginary cases:

29. John and Mary are newlyweds, and live in a small apartment in a high-rise block in the inner city. John works downtown. What factors probably influenced them to live in this kind of area? What are the advantages and disadvantages of such an area to them at this stage in their life cycle? What kind of neighbours will they have? Will they stay in such an area long?

30. After a decent interval, John and Mary have a child. What are the advantages and disadvantages now of their high-rise apartment in the inner city? Will they stay? If not, where may they move to? What may their new neighbours be like? Will they probably stay for a longer period in their new house than they did in their old apartment?

31. Fred and Wilma are a middle-aged couple living in their own three bedroom house in a 1930's suburb. Their children have recently married and left home. What factors might now influence them to move to a new residence? What kind of home in what kind of location might they choose?

32. Cathy and Heathcliffe live in a rented house with their two teenaged children. Heathcliffe is promoted to a better-paying position with his firm. Is the family likely to move house? What factors will they consider in moving, and to what part of the city will they probably move?

33. George and Martha own a large house in a suburban area. They discover that a new freeway will run almost through the bottom of their garden. How might they react to this news? Lawrence and Annie live in a small house in a working class district, also close to the route of the new freeway. Are they likely to react to the new road in the same way?

34. In questions 30-33, which moves were promoted by changes in the household status or the financial status of the family, and which by changes in the residential environment?

35. Make an informal survey of your class, and determine the families that have moved house in (a) the last 12 months, (b) the last two years, (c) the last 5 years. What proportion of the total class falls in each group? What proportion of the class has moved (a) at least once, (b) twice, (c) three times or more, in the last 5 years?

36. Ascertain the main reasons behind the moves of those members of the class who have moved house in the last year. Do these reasons fit into the three types of reasons suggested? If not, what other types of reasons are common?

The actual process of moving is quite complicated in a large city. What influences where a mover eventually lodges? We could say that every mover has a set of *objectives* in mind when moving, that is, he is looking for a house in an area that will satisfy certain needs, such as space, privacy, and aesthetic tastes. The nature of his old home may influence his objectives in that he may be looking in part for what the old home did not provide – for the extra bathroom, or the larger garden. The mover must operate within a set of *constraints* which are mainly financial or locational. The amount of money he has (or can borrow) and the distance he may conveniently be from critical points in the city such as his workplace, major amenities, or relatives, are critical. These may eliminate large parts of the city from serious consideration as potential new homesites, on the grounds of expense or remoteness. *Social* constraints are also important, since many people do not consider locating in new areas that are socially or ethnically in extreme contrast to their familiar location. Given these objectives and constraints, the mover will begin a more or less prolonged *search* for a new residence, using *information* collected from a variety of sources, including specialized sources (trade journals and real estate offices), and colloquial sources (friends and acquaintances); this last source is often important in finding new accommodation. Eventually the search narrows to an intensive examination and comparison of the few dwellings that come closest to the mover's objectives, within his constraints. Once a choice is made, the mover will be satisfied with the new house to the extent that it satisfies his objectives, or until he develops a new set of housing objectives.

37. Mr. Adams lives in a house marked X in Figure 6-12. The store where he works is marked Y. He wants to move to a new house to gain more space for his growing family. He wants a three-bedroom house and puts a value on open space and a quiet neighbourhood. He can't afford to spend more than $30,000, and he does not want to live more than half an hour's drive from work. What are Mr. Adam's objectives and constraints?

38. Mr. Adams uses the information in Figures 6-11 and 6-12 to help him find his new home. Which houses did he eliminate immediately? Why?

39. Houses 3, 6, 7, and 8 (marked on map) are possible choices for Mr. Adams on grounds of size and price. But which of these is he likely to eliminate next?

40. Probably you agree the final choice is between houses 6 and 3. What might the advantages be of choosing 6, in the same neighbourhood as the old house?

If Mr. Adams did, in fact, choose house 6, he acted quite typically. Most intra-urban residential moves are very short distance moves, over a few blocks, and within the same neighbourhood or to an adjacent one. Families rarely move to quite new parts of the city (to new geographical and social environments) in big jumps. Instead they tend to move gradually from one familiar environment to another.

1

UNIVERSITY AREA
$31,900

tremely attractive Southern
lonial style 3BR and den home
a quiet, safe cul-de-sac just a
ort walk from Shelbourne Ele-
ntary School. Gordon Head High
hool, the University and the
oquet Club. The existing large
per cent first mortgage can be
sumed and the vendor may
cept a very substantial second.
en to offers.
JOHN PLATT
386-7521 or 383-2700

2

SOUTH OAK BAY!!
GREENHOUSE TOO!!

A lovely older 2 bedroom home of
over 1100 sq. ft., featuring large
living room with fireplace, separate dining room. It does need a
little effort to bring it up to the
sparkling home you would be
proud to own, but take that into
consideration when making your
offer on the asking price of
$23,000. $14,000 financing is already on. For more information
contact:

3

ANOTHER
SOUTH OAK BAY
FAMILY HOME

Three bedroom with large
recreation or family room
in full basement. Separate
dining room. Fireplace in
comfortable living room.
Oak floors throughout.
Modern kitchen. Very pleasant, family home. For sale
at $24,900.

4

See this brand new 3 bdrm.
beauty with view of water &
mountains in choice location.
Close to beach at 528 Roslynn
Blvd. F.P. $36,000. Call Hank
Borman, 929-1591 or Harry
Taylor, 922-7968, or 988-6131.

5

ACANT!!

uick poss. - Lovely 2 bdrm.
on-bsmt. bungalow. 5 rms. 1,-
00 sq. ft. only 4 yrs. built on
ully landscaped 70' lot. Large
right kit. with Built-ins. Com-
ortable living rm. with fire-
lace. Complete storage space.
arport. hiktop parking. Vendor
ill carry balance with good
.P. F.P. $23,900. Call Mrs.
olmes 299-7375 or 324-2922.

EVERGREEN RLTY

6

$27,500
OWNER TRANSFERRED

An immaculate 7 yr. old cathedral
ent. bungalow. 18' L.R., D.R.,
arborite kitchen with nook. 3
bdrms. on main floor. High bsmt.
has panelled rec. rm. with f.p. and
washroom. Treed — 60x167 well
landscaped lot. A smart home in a
good area. Priced at $27,500 for
quick sale. Jack Gillmore. 988-
4078.

7

NEW HOME
$28,500

Rural setting on a large lot
(80x200). Construction almost completed and built with an eye to
quality and workmanship. 3 large
bedrooms. master en suite. a
kitchen with hand-crafted cabinets
that Madam will appreciate. L-
shape living and dining room and
overall approx. 1,280 sq. ft. The full
high basement has roughed-in
fireplace and plumbing. Many more
features so call now to view without
obligation.
388-4271 or 479-6648
Bill Anderson

8

Beautifully finished three-bedroom
home in the popular Colwood area.
Dining room with fireplace. Living
room plus chandelier and sliding
glass doors to sundeck. O bles of
cupboard space in the cab. elect.
kitchen plus range hood and space
for that breakfast table. Full bgt.
basement. large drive-in plus
roughed-in 4th bedroom or den plus
furnace room and workshop are.
plus family room space. Asking
$25,500 plus good financing.

Fig. 6-11 Housing information considered by Mr. Adams

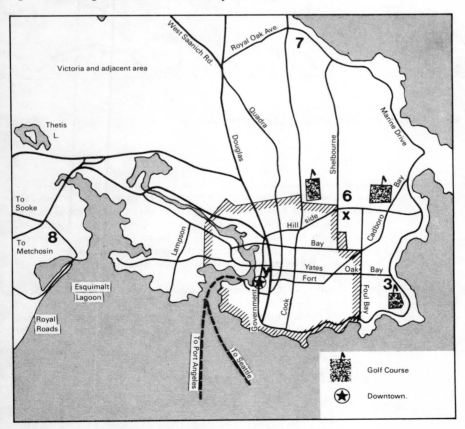

Fig. 6-12 Location of houses considered by Mr. Adams

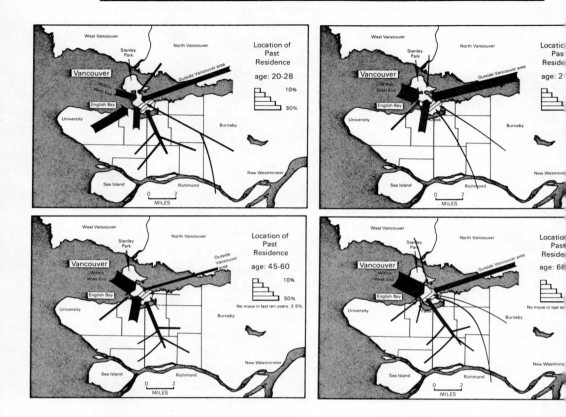

Fig. 6-13 Past residences of West End apartment dwellers

41. From Figure 6-13, estimate the percentage of people who moved into Vancouver's West End from previous residences (a) within the West End itself, (b) within the city of Vancouver, (c) outside the city of Vancouver, (d) outside the Vancouver area altogether (in each age group). How may you explain the variations in origins? Account for differences between age groups also. Which parts of the metropolitan area send very few people to the West End? Why?

42. Using a sample of your classmates, plot their present address on a city map, and their previous address. Are most of the moves "long distance" or "short distance" moves? What sources of information were considered by the families before a move was made? What was the most influential source of information?

5.   Movements Within the City

The residential areas we have described in a previous section and the functional areas we described in Part Five are not independent of one another. Rather they are connected by the regular movement of people; for example, the movement from residential areas to workplaces or to shopping centres, or the movement of people from one part of the city to another for social purposes.

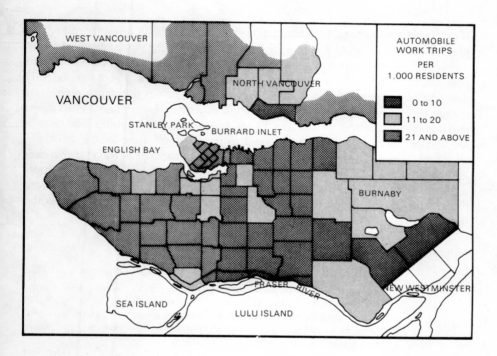

NUMBER OF AUTOMOBILE WORK-TRIPS TO THE CORE PER 1000
RESIDENTIAL POPULATION BY DISTANCE FROM DOWNTOWN.

DISTANCE FROM GEORGIA/GRANVILLE		NUMBER OF WORK-TRIPS
RING 1	(LESS THAN 1 MILE)	11.3 PER 1000
RING 2	(1.0 TO 1.9 MILES)	15.3 PER 1000
RING 3	(2.0 TO 2.9 MILES)	16.4 PER 1000
RING 4	(3.0 TO 3.9 MILES)	23.0 PER 1000
RING 5	(4.0 TO 4.9 MILES)	18.3 PER 1000
RING 6	(5.0 TO 5.9 MILES)	13.3 PER 1000
RING 7	(6.0 TO 6.9 MILES)	21.2 PER 1000
RING 8	(7.0 TO 7.9 MILES)	11.7 PER 1000
RING 9	(8.0 TO 8.9 MILES)	11.6 PER 1000
RING 10	(9.0 TO 9.9 MILES)	6.6 PER 1000
RING 11	(10.0 TO 10.9 MILES)	3.1 PER 1000

Fig. 6-14 Pattern of commuter traffic to downtown Vancouver

43. According to Figure 6-10, from what part of the city does downtown draw its workers? By referring to earlier maps in this part of the book, how may you explain this? (Figure 6-14 shows commuters by automobile. Would a map of the distribution of people who travel downtown to work by bus or other means be similar?) From the data in the table in Figure 6-14, construct a graph with commuters (per 1,000) on the vertical axis and distance to downtown on the horizontal axis. Plot the 11 rings as points on the graph. What does the graph tell you about the distribution of central area commuters in Vancouver? Try to explain the graph.

44. What problems can you anticipate in the movement of large numbers of people into the downtown area of a large city? From the map, what particular problems does Vancouver have?

Work journeys are regular in character. For example, in all cities there are two peaks a day of commuters moving to and from work. The demands of this peak movement on the urban transport system are great, and many cities are strained near breaking point at these times. Also particular work places consistently draw people from particular parts of the city. Thus places like downtown draw commuters from many parts of the city, but especially from middle class areas and apartment districts, since most downtown jobs are white collar jobs or jobs for women. Many industrial areas tend to draw people from nearby working class areas, since lower paid workers need to reduce the cost of travel by clustering close to their work place. However, modern suburban industrial districts where many workers arrive by car, can draw people from long distances across the city, if they are located on the circumferential freeways that cut across the outer city.

Social journeys are less regular than work journeys, but may show some patterning on inspection.

45. On a city map, locate your home. Over a period of about a week, locate the journeys you make, for school, for shopping, for social purposes. Do the journeys you make trace out a pattern of movement? Is there a local "neighbourhood" in which most of your trips begin and end, and where your regular needs are met?

46. Compare your *objective social space* map with that of an older and younger brother, or with that of an adult in your family. Do these *social maps* overlap? What can you say about the social space of the young and old? If you can, compare your family's maps with those of another family in another part of town. How do these maps compare? Do they overlap?

47. What characteristics of your neighbourhood influence the form of your social space? What changes could you suggest in your local area to make this social space more convenient? (More open space? Traffic segregation?)

In fact, when we examine the social space of many urbanites, we often find it revolves around a small area – a neighbourhood – within which most journeys begin and end, in which most needs are met, and which they come to know very well. For some people this can be a small area indeed; for the small child, the house and back streets; for the school child and housewife, a few nearby blocks around the school and local shops. Working adults go beyond this daily, and for them a familiar "corridor" connects the known home neighbourhood and work area. But for many people there are large areas of their own city that they may never visit.

48. Make a list of those parts of your city that you visit (a) often, (b) sometimes, (c) never. What is the nature of the areas you never visit? Which parts of the city might everyone in the city visit sooner or later?

49. Which of the parts of the city in the right-hand list are the kinds of people in the left-hand list likely to visit (a) often, (b) never.

1. middle class housewife	1. suburban high school
2. unskilled worker	2. downtown shopping district
3. pre-school child	3. waterfront industrial district
4. old age pensioner	4. public park
5. professional worker	5. downtown financial district
6. teenage student	6. upper class suburb.

50. What are the consequences and problems of the fact that much of the city is "unknown territory" to many of its inhabitants?

6.   An Exercise on Urban Growth

We can try to pull together our knowledge of the processes of urban development and of the factors that influence urban land use by attempting to recreate the growth of an imaginary but representative Canadian town. Drawing on the ideas and information of the previous sections (especially of Parts Two and Five) we should be able to build up, in a series of stages, a hypothetical city plan that is also realistic. Hopefully the exercise of creating an imaginary, but realistic, urban landscape will both fix the ideas discussed in our minds, and also convince us that these ideas go a long way towards explaining actual urban conditions.

Figure 6-15 shows the site of an imaginary city, as it might be just at the period of foundation of the city. A stream enters a large navigable river here, and early in the nineteenth century a small settlement develops around a grain mill set up to service the agricultural area to the north. Later in the century, a railway line is pushed through along the river bank, and the settlement is named by the railway as a maintenance stop.

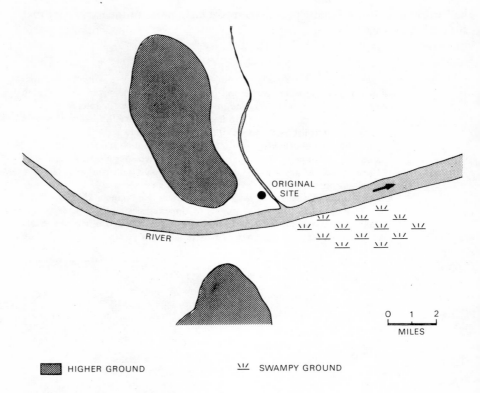

ORIGINAL
SITE

RIVER

O   1   2
MILES

HIGHER GROUND   SWAMPY GROUND

Fig. 6-15 A hypothetical urban site

51. In the later nineteenth century agricultural machinery, railway equipment, and food industries develop in the town. In which locations would they develop? Place these firms on the map (or a copy of it). What factors did you consider in locating these industries?

52. In the 1880's a streetcar system is built. Locate on your map the alignment of routes and location of stops. What factors influence your choice? What will be the effect on the future city growth of these alignments?

53. Shade on your map areas of upper class and lower class residences in the late nineteenth century. Why these areas?

54. Suppose the late nineteenth century sees a period of East European immigration. Where might the immigrant population congregate? Explain.

55. After World War I industrial growth continues with the growth of an electrical products industry and the expansion of the food industry. Where will these firms locate, and why? Put them on your map.

56. Shade the upper and lower class residential areas that grow up in the inter-war period. What probably happens to the older established residential areas at this time?

57. In the 1930's a new city hall is built. Where might this be located? Place it on your map with a distinctive symbol.

58. During World War II an aircraft plant and an army training camp are set up. Where might these be located? What would happen to these after the end of the war, with what effect on the subsequent form of the city?

In the 1950's and 1960's important transport changes occur. A bridge is built over the major river; the streetcar system is closed down as uneconomic; major improvements in highways are made to accommodate increased auto traffic, and a bypass freeway is built around the northern edge of the city. These changes, occurring rapidly after the hiatus caused by war greatly affect the form of the city in the next two decades.

59. In the 1950's and 1960's rapid growth also occurs. New manufacturing industries (engineering, electronics) develop and the old established food industries grow; this offsets the decline of the railway equipment industry. Locate these new industries on the map. Explain your choice. The city also becomes the site of the head office of a large insurance company. Locate this also and justify your choice.

60. Shade distinctively on the map the low density residential areas of the 1950's and 1960's, differentiating between upper and lower class areas. What will now be the nature of the older residential areas? Locate also the apartment growth of the last decade.

61. Locate on the map the two major shopping centres, the planned industrial estate, the new university, and the new airport developed in the 1960's. Explain your choice in each case.

62. In the late 1960's the city embarks on a campaign to beautify itself and increase its stock of recreational land. What areas are candidates for beautifying? What potential recreational sites remain in the city? What are the problems of claiming them for recreational use?

63. Indicate by arrows on the map the main direction of future growth of the city.

SEVEN

The Emerging City

1.   Introduction

As we move into the last quarter of the twentieth century, it is clear that we are also moving into an overwhelmingly urban world. Canada, like all other industrialized nations, will in future have a large proportion of its population concentrated in cities. More than this, a significant proportion of the population will be concentrated in a very few, very large cities – great metropolitan centres that will dominate the commercial, political, and cultural life of the nation, as centres of work, opinion, education, and fashion. Most of the important decisions affecting the world today are made in a few great cities. In Canada many more business and government decisions which affect the rest of the country are made in Toronto, Ottawa, and Montreal than in, say, Brantford, Moose Jaw, and Kamloops.

Moreover, as technology increases, travel and communication between these great cities becomes so easy that they operate as if they were one single city. Information flashes from city to city by telephone, telex, radio, and television as quickly and easily as it can go from point to point within a single city. Business meetings may be held between men in different cities, and decisions made in one place can be instantly acted upon in another. A Montreal businessman can leave his office in Place Ville Marie and a few hours later be in a conference room in Toronto's Royal York Hotel without once going into the open air. Increasingly, it is almost as easy to send people and ideas between the major cities as it is to send them between two buildings in the same city.

The great cities of the nation have certain common characteristics and problems. In this section, we will look in detail at some of the problems of our emerging metropolitan centres. In Part Eight, a selection of readings on the city will carry on this discussion and will add some new themes. Here, however, we shall discuss directly the question of the suburban growth of the large city – the situation of "growth by sprawl" common to many cities – and the problem of the merging of neighbouring cities into giant urbanized areas which is occurring in a few locations – for example, in southern Ontario. We will also discuss a problem of critical importance in large cities of today, the transport problem: moving thousands of people around a complex city for many purposes.

Fig. 7-1 Aerial view of Richmond, B.C., in 1963

Fig. 7-2 Aerial view of Richmond, B.C., in 1969

2.   The Growth of the Suburbs

Canada's first suburbs appeared in the early years of the century as streetcar lines were built out from the centres of the larger cities. In those days automobiles were rare curiosities and the streetcar was the only way that most people had of getting downtown, where the majority of jobs were concentrated. Once streetcar lines were built to outlying areas they encouraged residential growth there, for they made it as possible for people from these distant areas to travel downtown as people from areas within walking distance of the core. Thus, the earliest suburbs were strung out along the streetcar lines, and can often be distinguished even today as ribbons of older development, surrounded by that which has been built later. Often the streets which once carried streetcar tracks are now lined with stores, behind which the rows of older residences extend for a few blocks.

This pattern of suburban growth lasted until the more widespread use of the car brought about a complete change. When people no longer depended upon the streetcar, then land could be subdivided for residential use several miles from a city. At first it was only the rich who could afford to drive cars, and so the earliest suburbs of this kind consisted of large houses in spacious grounds. At this time winding tree-lined streets were fashionable and the suburbs which appeared – like Vancouver's Old Shaughnessy district, Calgary's Mount Royal, Toronto's Rosedale, or Montreal's Westmount – seemed to combine some of the advantages of the tranquillity of the countryside with accessibility to downtown. As we saw in Part Three, the town mansions which the wealthy left when they moved to the suburbs were often taken over by new immigrants to the city, and frequently became the poorest areas.

The exclusiveness of the suburbs really only ended when the majority of people could afford cars, an event to which both the mass-produced Model T Ford and increased prosperity contributed. It was this and the introduction of government support for housing in the mid-thirties that set the stage for the suburban explosion. Land speculators purchased relatively cheap farmland on the outer edges of cities and subdivided it for sale; most farmers were only too willing to receive from the developer more money than they could save in a lifetime of farming. Today many of our larger cities are surrounded by a disorganized suburban *sprawl*. To some this seems to combine the worst rather than the best of urban and rural life, and constitutes one of the major urban problems at the present time.

1. Figures 7-1 and 7-2 are views of the same area taken six years apart. Draw a map of the area at the same scale and show with different colours the part that was built up in 1963 and that which was added later. What factors might explain the more intense suburbanization of some parts of the area?
2. What replaced the race-track marked R in Figure 7-1?
3. Refer to Figure 4-4, which shows the shopping centre marked S in Figure 7-1. What was the previous use of the land behind the shopping centre before it was developed for residential use? What is the significance of the

fact that the houses in the background are of similar design?

4. What problems might be encountered in providing services of electricity, water supply, and sewers to these houses?

5. Do you think the land shown in the photographs is being developed in the best way? What improvements might be suggested?

Since residential developers wish to make as large a profit as possible, they purchase the cheapest land available to them. Consequently a developer will often not purchase land close to an area which has already been developed since the price of this may have risen in expectation of a sale. Instead, he will move further afield to farmland whose price has not risen, or at least has not risen as much. The results of this kind of leapfrogging are that the suburban subdivisions are very widely spread apart, and therefore more costly to service. At first this is not felt as a disadvantage, since when few houses exist minimal services like unpaved roads, poor street lighting, or septic tanks are feasible: once the density increases, however, they are not acceptable. Another result of leapfrogging is that farmland between residential development often falls out of use, as its owner awaits the right price before selling to developers.

Table 7-1   Essential Services for New Suburbs

Service	Proposed Requirement
Lot Services	
Local streets:	Paved roadway giving two moving lanes and one parking lane; at least one sidewalk, curbs, gutters, and storm sewers, depending on local circumstances.
Water supply:	A supply and distribution system, with no pipe smaller than 6″ diameter, giving volume and pressure adequate for domestic use, sprinkling, and fire-fighting.
Sewers:	A sanitary sewer system connected to a suitable treatment plant or outfall.
Street lighting:	An adequately designed system.
District Services	
Fire protection:	A firehall within about 2 miles by road.
Schools:	An elementary school within half a mile; an 8 to 10-room secondary school within 2 miles.
Park:	A 4 to 5-acre park-playground within one-third mile; a 25 to 30-acre district park within about 1 mile.
Bus service:	One round-trip per day within one-third mile of every home.

SOURCE: Lower Mainland Regional Planning Board of B.C., *Land for Living* (New Westminster, B.C., 1963).

6. Table 7-1 shows the essential services for new suburbs suggested by one Canadian planning authority. Suggest why the authority might consider each of these services essential. Which of these services would be difficult or costly to provide to an area like that shown in Figure 7-1? Why might a suburban municipality with few industries find it impossible to provide these services?

7. From a survey of the "Houses for Sale" column in your own newspaper:
   a) Locate on a map the major new subdivisions and find which of the ser-

Fig. 7-3 Bramalea, Ont.

vices listed above are provided.
b) Compare the price of houses in the suburbs with similar houses in the central area.

Without industry, suburban municipalities often cannot raise enough revenue from taxes to provide all the services they may wish to. Many have tried to attract industrial development, sometimes by providing industrial parks like that shown in Figure 5-6. Industry and business have both seen advantages in locating in the suburbs for, since land is cheaper there, they can afford to expand their premises much more than they could in the central city. To a certain extent, the suburbanization of business and industry has helped to ease the traffic problems of the large city, since when work is available locally fewer people have to commute to the central city. Nonetheless, to brave the morning and evening rush hours still seems to be one of the burdens of life for many suburbanites.

A solution to the problem of uncontrolled urban sprawl is that of constructing completely new towns as satellites to the major cities. Both Great Britain and Sweden have pioneered towns of this kind as public developments, and London, England is ringed by such new towns providing both residential accommodation and employment. In Canada, no comparable new towns have been developed as a public enterprise, but private developers have carried out similar projects, most notably in Bramalea, Ontario. This development was started in 1959 and ten years later contained a population of 16,000.

8. What different kinds of land use can be observed in Figure 7-3?

9. What distinguishes Bramalea from many other suburban developments? How does it differ from British or Swedish New Towns?

10. What evidence can you see in Figure 7-3 for the existence of schools, retail facilities, or other services? Why do the original farm field boundaries in the area not show as clearly in Bramalea as in Richmond?

11. How much variety would you expect there to be, from the evidence of Figure 7-3, in the social and economic status of Bramalea's residents? (Compare your answer with the excerpt on p. 158.).

12. What advantages and disadvantages do you think there would be to living in a satellite town like Bramalea?

3.   The Golden Horseshoe—A Canadian Megalopolis

In the more highly urbanized parts of the world the sprawling suburbs of adjoining towns have come together so that it sometimes seems as though no open country remains to separate one urban centre from another. This development was first observed in the industrial Midlands of Great Britain and in London, where vast urban areas were given the name *conurbations*. Such conurbations exist today in many parts of the world, and especially in Western Europe, Japan, and the United States. Along the northeastern seaboard of the United States in particular, not only have the previously separate urban centres of Boston, New York, Philadelphia, Baltimore, and Washington and the many smaller cities grown together physically, but also their economic lives are so closely interwoven that in some respects they operate as a single city. This is the area which is known today as *Megalopolis* since it is evidently both larger and more complicated than a single metropolis. Its influence is felt not only throughout the United States, but throughout the world, for it is here that many of the really important decisions affecting the world's economy are made.

In Canada a somewhat similar region is to be found curving along the western end of Lake Ontario from Toronto to Hamilton. Though nowhere nearly as large as its United States counterpart, the Golden Horseshoe, as it is called, does exert as strong an influence over the life of Canada as Megalopolis does over that of the United States. Above all this is the centre of Canadian wealth and influence, as well as of much industrial activity.

Some evidence of the area's rapid industrial growth may be found in Figure 7-4. We learned in Part Two that this area experienced some of the earliest growth in Canada, as steel mills were established at Hamilton. To the early advantages of accessibility to water and rail transportation and a central location has now been added that of accessibility to a large and growing market. It is obviously an advantage to be able to manufacture many products as close as

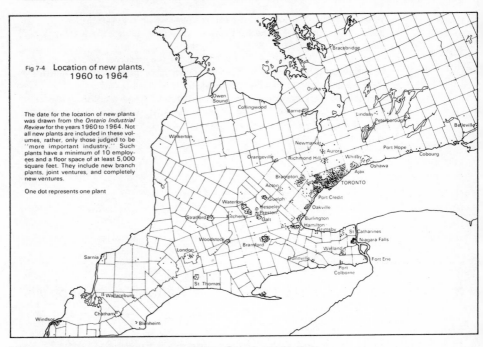

Fig. 7-4 Location of new plants in southern Ontario, 1960-1964

Fig. 7-5 Counties of southern Ontario

possible to their consumers, and so the Golden Horseshoe's large and relatively rich population has attracted a great number of industries. About one-third of the purchasing power of the entire country is actually found within a one-hundred-mile radius of Toronto, and so this area is attractive to many manufacturers who wish to be close to a large consumer market. Cars, computers, clothing, food products, and many other manufactured goods are produced in this area. Industrial growth means population growth also, and eventually changes of other kinds.

In order to examine how these changes differ from one area to another, geographers and other social scientists often construct maps based upon statistics taken from the census. When statistical information is shown on a map rather than in a table, patterns emerge which either answer questions, or cause us to ask questions about the differences between areas. We have suggested that the Golden Horseshoe differs in several important respects from the rest of southern Ontario, and in particular that it contains the greatest concentration of industry and commerce. What other characteristics follow from this may be clear by looking at maps showing a number of different demographic features. In the following exercises, we shall use statistical data to draw our own maps rather than examining those which someone else has drawn for us. The exercises need not be unduly laborious if the work is divided among a whole class rather than being done by individual effort.

13. Trace or photocopy from Figure 7-5 three outline maps of southern Ontario showing county boundaries.
14. Using Table 7-2 calculate the following factors for each county.
    a) The percentage increase in population between 1956 and 1966; i.e.,
    $$\frac{\text{Pop. in 1966} - \text{Pop. in 1956}}{\text{Pop. in 1956}} \times 100\%$$
    b) The percentage of the population which was urban in 1966: i.e.,
    $$\frac{\text{Urban population in 1966}}{\text{Total population in 1966}} \times 100\%$$
    c) The percentage of the rural population which was non-farm in 1966: i.e.,
    $$\frac{\text{Non-farm population in 1966}}{\text{Rural population in 1966}} \times 100\%$$
    (These percentages may be calculated quickly if each member of the class takes only one or two counties.)
15. Show the way in which the rate of population increase has varied from one part of southern Ontario to another by shading those counties in which the increase was:
    a) greater than the provincial average of 29 per cent, in a dark shade;
    b) between 14 and 29 per cent, in a medium shade;
    c) between 6 and 14 per cent, in a light shade; and
    d) less than 6 per cent, unshaded.
16. Show the variation in the urbanization of southern Ontario by indicating with a different shade those counties in which the percentage of the population which was urban in 1966 was:
    a) greater than 80;
    b) between 50 and 80; and
    c) less than 50.
17. Show the variation in the percentage of the rural population which did not

Table 7-2   Populations of Ontario counties, 1956 and 1966

County	Total Pop. (1956)	Total Pop. (1966)	Urban (1966)	Rural (1966) Total	Non-Farm	Farm
ONTARIO (province)	5,404,933	6,960,870	5,593,440	1,367,430	885,735	481,695
Brant	77,992	90,945	69,529	21,416	14,149	7,267
Bruce	42,070	43,085	15,836	27,249	11,281	15,968
Carleton	282,630	407,463	375,969	31,494	22,139	9,355
Dufferin	15,569	17,108	6,942	10,166	3,673	6,493
Dundas	16,978	17,106	5,787	11,319	4,771	6,548
Durham	35,827	44,549	21,967	22,582	14,067	8,515
Elgin	59,114	61,912	30,062	31,850	19,429	12,421
Essex	246,901	280,922	232,276	48,646	29,780	18,866
Frontenac	76,534	97,138	71,540	25,598	19,068	6,530
Glengarry	18,693	18,181	2,864	15,317	8,373	6,944
Grenville	20,563	23,429	9,305	14,124	9,631	4,493
Grey	60,971	62,592	30,972	31,620	12,646	18,974
Haldimand	26,067	30,020	11,327	18,693	10,439	8,254
Haliburton	8,012	7,768	—	7,768	7,021	747
Halton	68,297	140,800	131,477	9,323	6,008	3,315
Hastings	83,745	94,127	63,903	30,224	19,737	10,487
Huron	51,728	54,446	22,366	32,080	12,766	19,314
Kent	85,362	96,406	57,444	38,962	21,786	17,176
Lambton	89,939	108,236	75,116	33,120	17,273	15,847
Lanark	38,025	41,212	23,810	17,402	10,542	6,860
Leeds	43,077	49,129	25,505	23,624	15,403	8,221
Lennox and Addington	21,611	25,202	6,648	18,554	12,593	5,961
Lincoln	111,740	146,099	117,274	28,825	15,226	13,599
Manitoulin	11,060	10,544	1,441	9,103	6,355	2,748
Middlesex	190,897	249,403	209,291	40,112	20,782	19,330
Muskoka	25,134	27,691	9,644	18,047	16,555	1,492
Nipissing	60,452	73,533	46,386	27,147	23,166	3,981
Norfolk	46,122	50,578	19,031	31,547	17,608	13,939
Northumberland	38,018	45,074	20,291	24,783	15,707	9,076
Ontario	108,440	170,818	139,652	31,166	20,508	10,658
Oxford	65,228	76,018	42,236	33,782	17,476	16,306
Parry Sound	28,095	28,335	8,120	20,215	16,985	3,230
Peel	83,108	172,321	149,534	22,787	16,487	6,300
Perth	55,057	60,424	35,837	24,587	7,851	16,736
Peterborough	67,981	81,959	61,886	20,073	13,225	6,848
Prescott	26,291	27,155	13,313	13,842	6,545	7,297
Prince Edward	21,145	21,307	6,314	14,993	9,810	5,183
Renfrew	78,245	89,453	54,754	34,699	23,661	11,038
Russell	18,994	21,107	5,892	15,215	8,079	7,136
Simcoe	127,016	149,132	91,077	58,055	38,707	19,348
Stormont	56,452	59,550	45,766	13,784	8,055	5,729
Victoria	28,248	30,917	14,745	16,172	8,643	7,529
Waterloo	148,774	216,728	186,922	29,806	18,369	11,437
Welland	149,606	178,818	149,776	29,042	22,677	6,365
Wellington	75,691	94,177	66,072	28,105	12,257	15,848
Wentworth	316,238	394,299	356,839	37,460	28,742	8,718
York	1,440,601	2,018,019	1,973,424	44,595	34,445	10,150

SOURCE: Dominion Bureau of Statistics, *Census of Canada*, 1956 and 1966.

make its living by farming in 1966. In this case choose your own system of shading.

18. What do your maps suggest about the Golden Horseshoe compared with the rest of southern Ontario? Which other counties seem to share similar characteristics to those of the Golden Horseshoe? Why?

19. Referring to Figure 7-4, where have most new plants located in southern Ontario in the period 1960-1964? What advantages does this area have for new industries?

20. Make a list of all the factors which you think might also distinguish the Golden Horseshoe from the rest of southern Ontario.

The effects of the features you have shown on your map may be observed on the landscape itself. As more people move into the Golden Horseshoe, its character changes from rural to urban, and much of its productive agricultural land is taken up for residential use like that shown in Figure 7-6. This then is suburban development with a difference. Like that of the United States Megalopolis, it is related not so much to one city as to a complex of cities. Even the land which remains agricultural changes its use as it increasingly comes to supply the enormous needs of the urban population for perishable commodities like milk and fresh vegetables. Thus either through actual residential development, or through changing agricultural land use, the entire surrounding area has fallen under the influence of the growing, merging cities.

21. In Figure 7-6, what changes have occurred in land use? What evidence is there that these changes have probably been quite recent?

22. Find the location shown in Figure 7-6, the Niagara peninsula, on an atlas map. Where would the residents of the houses shown in the photograph probably find employment?

Fig. 7-6 Residential land use in the Niagara peninsula

Table 7-3   Population of Canadian Provinces and Largest Cities, 1961 and 1969

	Provincial Population			Population of Largest City	
	1961	1969		1961	1969
Manitoba	921,686	977,000	Metro. Winnipeg ..	475,989	528,600
British Columbia ..1,629,082		2,056,000	Metro. Vancouver	790,165	978,100
Quebec 5,259,211		5,976,000	Metro. Montreal ..2,109,509		2,563,800
Ontario 6,236,092		7,425,000	Metro. Toronto 1,824,481		2,329,200
Alberta 1,331,944		1,553,000	Metro. Edmonton..	337,568	437,700
Nova Scotia	737,007	764,000	Metro. Halifax	183,946	205,600
Newfoundland	457,853	513,000	Metro. St. John's..	90,838	107,600
Prince Edward Is...	104,692	110,000	Charlottetown	18,318	18,500
New Brunswick	597,936	626,000	Metro. Saint John	95,563	102,500
Saskatchewan	925,181	961,000	Regina	112,141	139,200

SOURCE: 1961 figures from Dominion Bureau of Statistics, *Census of Canada, 1961.*
1969 figures from *Financial Post, Survey of Markets, 1969.*

This metropolitanization of the population is not only taking place in Ontario, of course. In nearly every Canadian province an increasingly large proportion of the total population is congregating in a few large cities. Table 7-3 shows this, but also shows that the degree of concentration is not the same in every province.

23. Using Table 7-3, calculate the percentage of the population in each province which is concentrated in the largest city, at each date. Arrange the provinces in order, from the highest to lowest percentage, at each date. How might you explain this ranking?

24. Identify the provinces where the share of the largest city has increased, and where it has decreased over the period. Is the general trend one of increasing concentration of population in the largest cities? If so, how might you explain this trend? Identify and explain those provinces that show different trends.

4.   Transportation Problems

Most major Canadian cities experienced their formative growth from the mid-nineteenth to the early twentieth centuries. At this period, the major forms of urban transport were walking, horse-drawn vehicles, and the electric streetcar. As previously mentioned, these forms of transport encouraged the development of a densely settled central city with ribbons of residential development extending outwards along the street car lines.

Fig. 7-7 Downtown Toronto at the turn of the century

25. How many different kinds of transport can you see in the photograph? For what purposes may the various types of transport have been used? (Goods delivery, personal travel, and so on.)
26. From the photograph, what kinds of traffic problems may turn-of-the-century Toronto have experienced? (Consider other times of the year than that shown on the photograph.)

From the 1920's, as the prosperity of the urban populations grew, the motor vehicle became an increasingly important form of urban transportation, and by the late 1950's it had become the dominant form of transport in North American cities. By this time the automobile and truck had completely replaced horse-drawn vehicles and steam tractors for the movement of people and goods (and almost eliminated walking!), and motor buses were on the way to eliminating streetcars as the major form of public transport.

27. What is the percentage increase in automobile registrations in Toronto over the period 1954-1962, from Figure 7-8? What is the percentage decline in transit ridership?
28. How may you explain the great increase in automobile use shown in Figure 7-8? What are the advantages of the automobile, truck, and bus over other forms of urban transport?

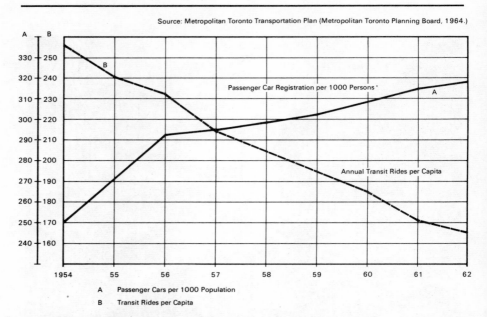

Source: Metropolitan Toronto Transportation Plan (Metropolitan Toronto Planning Board, 1964.)

Fig. 7-8 Increase in passenger car registration and decline in transit ridership in Toronto, 1954-1962

The impact of the automobile on the form of the modern city has, of course, been great. The new mode of transport has allowed the open sectors between residential corridors to be filled in, and broad new areas up to twenty or thirty miles from the central city have been brought within commuting range, and so opened for residential development. Industries have been able to develop in new locations in the suburbs and along highways, and from these locations can now serve a variety of markets. Planned shopping centres have grown up in outer areas to almost rival downtown. The car and truck offer convenience (door to door movement and constant availability), flexibility (a variety of cargoes can be carried over many forms of road surface), comfort (air conditioning and radios), reliability (little affected by weather or strikes), plus relatively good speed and cost characteristics. No wonder they have become dominant, and forced the city to adapt to their needs, moulding urban forms around them!

In fact, in most North American cities, over three-quarters of the households now have at least one car, and in some cities up to a third of all households have two cars. It should not surprise us to learn that in many North American cities over 70 per cent of all trips are made by automobile. For example:

In central Los Angeles	75% of all travel is by auto
In suburban Los Angeles	86% of all travel is by auto
In central Fort Worth	80% of all travel is by auto
In suburban Fort Worth	88% of all travel is by auto
In central Detroit	68% of all travel is by auto
In suburban Detroit	86% of all travel is by auto
In central Philadelphia	42% of all travel is by auto

In suburban Philadelphia   70% of all travel is by auto
In central Boston   38% of all travel is by auto
In suburban Boston   67% of all travel is by auto
In Toronto   66% of all travel is by auto

SOURCE: W. Owen, *The Metropolitan Transportation Problem,* (New York: Anchor Books, 1966) p. 30, and Metropolitan Toronto Planning Board, *Metropolitan Toronto Transportation Plan* (Toronto, 1964).

29. Explain the central-suburban differences in the relative importance of the automobile in the above cities.
30. Explain the variations in the importance of the automobile among the cities, especially the lower proportions in the large eastern cities. Who are the people who are *not* travelling by automobile?
31. From what you know of the following Canadian cities, in which would you expect the automobile to be relatively more important as a mode of transport: (a) Vancouver, (b) Edmonton, (c) Montreal, (d) Toronto, (e) Halifax, (f) Quebec City.
32. How many different kinds of transport can you see in Figure 7-9? How may the various types of transport you can see be used?
33. From the photograph, what kinds of traffic problems may twentieth-century Toronto be facing? What modifications has the automobile forced onto the downtown area?
34. Compare Figures 7-7 and 7-9. Do the traffic problems of downtown seem worse now than 60 years ago? What particular problems has extensive automobile use brought to cities?

Although the automobile and truck have become the dominant form of urban transport because of the advantages they offer, they have also forced some painful readjustments on cities. The millions of vehicular trips that a large city generates every week cannot easily be made over a street system inherited from the nineteenth century. It is not only that 20 people in 20 cars take up more highway space than 20 people in a streetcar, but also that the affluent urbanite now makes more trips per week than he did in the past. Extra time, money, and the availability of a car have increased the *trip generating capacity* of urban households recently, and this, as well as the change to a more space consuming mode of travel, adds to urban traffic problems.

The traffic problem of the large modern city then is to cope with the tremendous demand for movement from households and businesses, where many of these trips are by automobile, and where the street system is inadequate to handle them. An extra problem is that travel tends to be concentrated into two periods of the day in all cities – *peak periods* – as Figure 7-10 clearly shows.

35. From Figure 7-10, what percentages of all trips in Toronto are made in the periods 7 A.M.–10 A.M. and 4 P.M.–7 P.M.? What percentage of automobile trips is made in these periods and what percentage of transit trips? Explain the difference.
36. What is the nature of the peak-period movement? Does the graph show more trips in the afternoon than in the morning period? Why should this be so?

Fig. 7-9 Downtown Toronto today

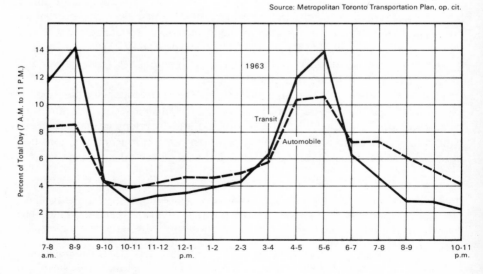

Fig. 7-10 Daily traffic flow in Toronto

37. Would a graph of daily movements over a weekend period show patterns of peaking? If so, locate and explain the peaks.
38. What problems may be associated with this "peaking" of urban traffic?

The traffic peaks typical of the weekday movement patterns of any large city are of course the morning and evening "rush hours" when commuters are travelling to and from work. The journey to work, concentrated as it is into this time of day, is the most important element in the daily flow of traffic in the city. In a large city like Toronto, 60 per cent of all trips are work trips. Social and recreational trips typically account for about 15 per cent of all trips and shopping trips about 10 per cent; business trips and trips for other purposes make up the remainder. However, as the leisure and income of urban families increase, it is likely that recreational trips will increase in number and relative importance. New traffic peaks – and new congestion problems – may develop at weekends on highways leading out of the city to major parks or resort areas.

The major difficulty of the peaked character of urban movement is the need for large and elaborate transport systems to carry the peak load for relatively short periods of time; the system may then be under-used at other periods of the day or at weekends. The system is usually jammed to capacity at the peak periods, with great costs in vehicle wear and tear, lost time and lost patience. One possible solution is to "stagger" work hours to reduce the work journey component of the peak period, and thus reduce the pressure on congested transport facilities at these times, spreading the load more evenly through the day.

5. Towards Solving the Metropolitan Transport Problem

Given the difficulties of moving large numbers of people about within extensive urban areas, a number of solutions have been proposed. Some of these are *engineering* solutions; they involve building more physical facilities to move more people at higher speeds. To date, the commonest proposal is *urban freeways*. Freeways have existed between cities in North America since the 1930's. In the 1950's, freeways were brought inside the city, to help solve the problem of internal city movement. Now most large American cities have many miles of urban freeway, as shown in Table 7-4.

Table 7-4   Miles of Freeway in Selected North American Cities, Completed or under Construction, 1964-1965

Boston	288 miles	San Francisco	314 miles
Chicago	341 miles	Philadelphia	242 miles
Dallas	164 miles	Toronto	93 miles
Detroit	162 miles	Montreal*	83 miles
Los Angeles	459 miles	Vancouver*	55 miles
New York	899 miles	Ottawa*	17 miles

*as of 1965

SOURCE: W. Owen, *op. cit.*, p. 55; *Metropolitan Toronto Transportation Plan, op. cit.*, and Norman D. Lea, *Toward Understanding Urban Transportation* (Toronto, n.d.), p. 27.

---

40. Can you explain the variations in miles of freeway built or under construction in the cities in Table 7-4?
41. What are the advantages and drawbacks of an extensive urban freeway system?

Certainly the urban freeway alleviates aspects of the transport problem. It speeds up travel between certain points in the city; for example, between downtown and certain suburban communities. Circumferential freeways that circle the city help crosstown commuting and reroute traffic around instead of through the congested central city. The freeway helps segregate through traffic from local traffic, and takes the pressure off arterial roads and residential streets so that these become safer and more pleasant for local driving and shopping, and delivery and service activities are facilitated. However, the freeway "solution" also has its own drawbacks. Firstly, it is very expensive. For example:

In Los Angeles	10 miles of freeway cost	$ 5.5 million per mile
In New York	5 miles of freeway cost	22.45 million per mile
In Philadelphia	20 miles of freeway cost	7.5 million per mile
In Boston	3 miles of freeway cost	41.67 million per mile
In Chicago	8 miles of freeway cost	6.25 million per mile

SOURCE: W. Owen, *op. cit.* p. 44 (based on costs in mid-1950's).

---

42. Why might you expect the costs of urban freeway building to be high? Why do they vary from city to city?

The high cost of acquiring land in built up areas, the high cost of construction of the six- and eight-lane freeways needed to carry the heavy traffic, the high cost of ramps and elevated sections to cross existing streets, all add to urban freeway costs. The costs tend to be highest of all in the central parts of the older eastern cities, hence the almost astronomical cost of constructing the short length of freeway in central Boston, shown in the table above.

A second drawback with urban freeways is that they are disruptive of large

Fig. 7-11 The Macdonald-Cartier Freeway, Toronto

sections of the city. To build them, demolition of business districts and residential communities is often necessary. Once built, they are apt to be unpleasant to look at, to blight the neighbouring areas, to cut off one part of the city from the other. Debates over freeway alignments are now regular occurences in large cities. Threading a freeway through a crowded city without disrupting it is more difficult than passing a camel through the needle's eye!

Should the great road be finished or stopped in its tracks? Here are the arguments of the opposing sides

The Spadina expressway war is on again.

This week two Toronto mayoralty candidates, Controller Margaret Campbell and Liberal party hopeful Stephen Clarkson, promised to stop the $220 million expressway right in its tracks.

Immediately, the expressway, which has provoked more controversy than any other issue in Metro's 16-year history, once again became the hottest and most emotional issue in a hitherto quiet and somewhat lacklustre campaign.

Construction of the six-lane $135 million super road, with an $85 million facility for subway trains down the centre, is still proceeding towards its scheduled completion in 1975.

The city opposition will, however, be able to muster up the same powerful arguments which have been used since 1962 when Metro Council, after Frederick Gardiner in his last night as Metro chairman kept them sitting until 5 a.m., finally approved the project.

Since then, a small army of planners and urban experts have warned about the drastic effects the Spadina expressway will have on the city.

Most prominent among them is Jane Jacobs, an internationally known American expert on big city problems, who moved to Toronto a year ago.

Mrs. Jacobs, author of two widely respected books, The Death and Life of Great American Cities and The Economy of Cities, says the Spadina expressway "is the single greatest menace to the city."

"Toronto is going to be destroyed within another 15 years by the building of the expressway," she predicts.

For one thing, it will create "the most awful traffic jam in the whole world" where traffic is scheduled to pour out onto Spadina Rd. one block south of Bloor St.

The inevitable consequence of those traffic jams will be construction of even more expressways, such as the proposed Crosstown expressway, says Mrs. Jacobs.

"The whole dense part of the city will be sacrificed to expressways and parking lots," says Mrs. Jacobs. And the cars and the parking lots mean disruption of residential neighborhoods, wholesale bulldozing of homes, more noise and more pollution.

However, with Metro having already spent about $58 million on the project and with no hope of rolling up the existing one mile of concrete, expressway critics realize they'll have to live with at least part of it.

Proponents of the expressway will rely on Metro transportation and traffic experts, chiefly Metro's streets and traffic commissioner, Sam Cass, to present their case.

Cass can and will present some powerful arguments about why his expressway is not only necessary but really will be the most beautiful one in North America.

He immediately hits back hard at those protest meetings where the cry goes out to stop the expressway at Eglinton or St. Clair.

The protesters are really only protecting their own interests, investments and neighborhoods and are simply putting cars on streets near other people's homes farther uptown, Cass contends.

But even worse, says Cass, the whole purpose of the Spadina expressway is destroyed by halting it short of its goal.

Several detailed drivers' surveys over the years have shown that the expressway is needed to relieve the present traffic jams on north-south arteries, like Bathurst, Dufferin, Keele Sts. and Weston Rd., says Cass.

Stop the Spadina and those streets as well as several other cross streets will continue to be congested, he says.

In fact, Cass says, the Spadina expressway will be beautiful. Three tunnels, running under parks, will remove the cars from sight for a good part of the expressway and the rest will be depressed at least 20 feet below ground level.

SOURCES John Zaritsky, *Toronto Daily Star* (November 1, 1969).

---

43. In the newspaper article, what arguments are apparently being raised against the proposed freeway? Do you think the arguments sound valid? Do you think that all the facts necessary to make a considered judgement on the issue are covered in the article?
44. In Figure 7-11, what evidence can you see of the disruption of residential areas by the freeway? What efforts have apparently been made to reduce the impact of the freeway on neighbouring areas?

The final problem with the freeway solution is that any section, once built, gives only short term relief. The new section only attracts traffic to itself from nearby streets, encourages more trips to be made, and finally bogs down in worse congestion than before. In Toronto, four-lane freeways built a decade ago are now inadequate and must be widened to eight or twelve lanes. This is clearly undesirable if carried to extremes.

An alternate engineering solution is to move towards *mass transit* instead

Fig. 7-12 Toronto Rapid Transit System

of freeways. This is an attempt to arrest the decline in transit usage illustrated in Figure 7-8 by providing fast, modern service at low cost to the user. Usually the transit system focusses on downtown, and aims to serve the downtown commuter. The hope is to entice enough commuters away from automobiles so that peak hour congestion is reduced, and with it, downtown noise and pollution. It is hoped that expensive, disruptive freeways are curtailed by the provision of transit facilities. A variety of mass transit systems are available. One system is the partially underground electric railway (subway) which may be expensive to build but is not disruptive of the city fabric. Some cities have chosen this option. In the United States, San Francisco is spending one billion dollars on the Bay Area Rapid Transit System. In Canada, both Montreal and Toronto have recently built, at great capital cost, central transit systems.

46. From the map, what appear to be the functions of the Toronto Rapid Transit System? How does it compete with or complement the freeway system?

47. From the photograph, what are the advantages of the underground subway system?

Fig. 7-13 The Métro subway system in Montreal

Other mass transit systems include surface railways (used in New York and Boston), high speed buses in special lanes on freeways (as in Atlanta), or more exotic systems such as monorails or cushioncraft (not in operation yet). Each system has its own advantages, to do with flexibility, construction and operation costs, degree of urban disruption, degree of air pollution, all weather reliability, and so on.

---

48. Make a list of the relative advantages and disadvantages of the following mass transit systems: (a) underground railway, (b) surface railway, (c) high speed buses on segregated roadways, (d) monorails, (e) cushioncraft. Do any of these seem particularly suited for your town?

One point all these systems have in common is that they only make sense for large towns, say, metropolitan areas of at least one half to one million people. Smaller towns do not generate enough traffic even at peak hours to support a mass transit system. Also, these systems work best where the density of population is fairly high in suburban areas; this places larger numbers of people within the "catchment areas" of the stations, and makes it more likely that use of the system would be high enough for fairly efficient operation. Thus, a mass transit system tends to work best in, and will encourage the development of, centrally organized and more densely populated cities. The automobile in contrast tends to work best in, and favour the development of, multi-centred, low density cities. When cities choose one form of transport system over another, they go a long way towards choosing one basic form of city over another, so great is the interaction between transport and urban form.

An important point is that a good mass transit system in a large city may be of critical importance to the poorer and the older populations of the city. These are the people who cannot afford to own a car or who cannot drive one. In the past, as the automobile has risen to dominance, and transit ridership has declined, so the cost and service aspects of transit have also deteriorated, leaving the poor and old in worse plight than before. In the modern city, these people are less mobile than ever, in contrast with the highly mobile car owners. Finding employment and using city services is made extra difficult for those already disadvantaged. Thus improving the mass transit system of the city is a way to increase the opportunities open to the poor and old, as well as a way of reducing traffic congestion faced by commuters.

In fact, there is not a clear "either/or" choice between freeways and mass transit as solutions to the traffic problem. Most larger Canadian cities are opting for a mixture of both, and are trying to benefit from American experience in making their decisions.

A final point concerns the possibility of an *economic,* not an engineering, attack on the traffic problem. This is through so-called *road-pricing:* charging motorists for the use of streets in certain congested parts of the city. Instead of building and maintaining bridges and streets out of general taxes or bond issues, as at present, and then allowing all people to use them at no extra cost, it is suggested that a charge be made against the users of, say, downtown streets. Faced with an extra cost in travelling downtown by car a commuter might travel there by bus instead; only those people who really needed to go downtown by car would continue to do so, and many "unnecessary" car trips would be eliminated. The existing street system would not need to be expensively enlarged, if it had to cope with fewer automobile trips. This is an appealing approach, but a politically delicate one!

EIGHT

Urban Prospects:
A Collection of Readings

---

1.   Introduction

By now, we should have an increased understanding of the modern Canadian city. We should now be able to make more informed judgements about the problems of urban living, and how these problems affect us as citizens. We recognize, for example, that the city is a very complicated mechanism, the separate parts of which are related in quite subtle ways. A change in one may produce quite radical consequences elsewhere. A freeway can disrupt an existing community, a new shopping centre might hasten the decline of an established retail district or of the downtown area. Understanding the links between apparently different aspects of the city helps us to form our opinions about the way our cities are being governed and are growing. If one of the purposes of becoming educated is to be an informed citizen, then a result of having studied the city in some depth should be an increased ability to participate in the creation of urban environment with extra understanding.

The following pages pick up and elaborate some of the topics and themes we have discussed in earlier sections of this book. They contain a small sample of some of the body of literature on the city. Some of the readings reproduced here are concerned with feelings and with intuitive interpretations of the city. We shall examine a few excerpts from some novels set in the city, from which we can derive an understanding which goes beyond that of factual description. We shall examine also some of the social and environmental problems of the modern city which affect us all in one way or another. Crime and juvenile delinquency, poverty, ethnic discrimination, drug addiction and alcoholism, air and water pollution are not specifically urban problems, but all tend to be more intense and serious in urban centres. Finally, we shall look at some of the problems brought about by the so-called urban explosion; we shall consider the ways in which the city might grow, and the changes that might occur in the urban environment in the future.

2.   The Artist and the City

Our appreciation of the nature of the city and of city life does not come only from the work of social scientists. Novelists, artists, and journalists add their intuitive insights to our store of understanding. In their own way they confirm and enrich the data that the academic scholars build up by other methods of enquiry. The artist often helps us appreciate situations from the inside, so we can also come to know what the various circumstances of city life mean for the people who experience them.

Being by nature a country person, cities tend to bug me under any circumstances. Now, for the first time in my life, I am living totally on my own in a city strange to me. The city is Toronto – if it were New York, I would no doubt have flipped my lid after one week. As it is, things are bizarre enough. I do not drive a car, and with my oddly faulty sense of direction, finding my way around by public transport is slightly traumatic in itself. Then again, I am going in to an office (my own office – ye gods) for the first time in nearly 20 years.

. . . Walking alone in a city, when one is unaccustomed, has an element of madness and unreality. I have not yet relearned what every city dweller has to do in self-protection – that is, to block out of sight and hearing some of the zoom and flash and screech and rush and buzz and boing and shove and clatter. Still, all this I needed to know. And at least it means I'm viewing things with different eyes and ears than they will be in a month or so, when I'll look back and wonder how everything could have seemed so weird.

Adjustment, or whatever it is – learning the simplest rules of survival perhaps – begins to happen, it seems to me, in pendulum sweeps. One moment the impersonality of the city oppresses me as though I were breathing in some mind-numbing gas. The next moment the ability of people to maintain life as themselves seems nothing short of miraculous. We are a hell of a tough breed, after all – scathed, beatup, but tough. The wonder is not that so many crack up but that so many don't.

Morning subway, and there are no songs here, not even sad ones. Hundreds of eyes, focused on train floors, not on each other. Are floors safer to look at? Eglinton Davisville St. Clair Summerhill (nostalgically named) Rosedale and change at Bloor Tumult of hurtling anonymous bodies along the early platforms in the subterranean caves of ice masquerading as concrete or false marble, caves of chill, filled with hot lung-used air. All of us ascending escalators like one corporate octopus body, as on a conveyor belt taking us to a destination which may well turn out to be a meat factory run by human-devouring extra-terrestrial cacti.

Margaret Laurence, "Love and Madness in the City," *Vancouver Sun,* November 15, 1969.

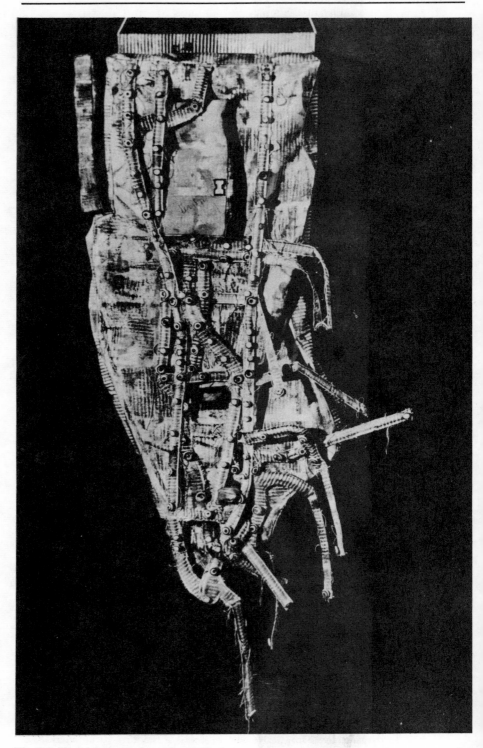

Fig. 8-1 "Soft Manhattan" by Claes Oldenburg

... They had come out on Lenox Avenue, though their destination was on Seventh; and nothing they passed was unfamiliar because everything they passed was wretched. It was not hard to imagine that horse carriages had once paraded proudly up this wide Avenue and ladies and gentlemen, ribboned, beflowered, brocaded, plumed, had stepped down from their carriages to enter these houses which time and folly had so blasted and darkened. The cornices had once been new, had once gleamed as brightly as now they sulked in shame, all tarnished and despised. The windows had not always been blind. The doors had not always brought to mind the distrust and secrecy of a city long besieged. At one time people had cared about these houses – that was the difference; they had been proud to walk on this Avenue; it had once been home, whereas now it was prison.

Now, no one cared: this indifference was all that joined this ghetto to the mainland. Now, everything was falling down and the owners didn't care; no one cared. The beautiful children in the street, black-blue, brown, and copper, all with a gray ash on their faces and legs from the cold wind, like the faint coating of frost on a window or a flower, didn't seem to care that no one saw their beauty. Their elders, great, trudging, black women, lean, shuffling men, had taught them, by precept or example, what it meant to care or not to care: whatever precepts were daily being lost, the examples remained, all up and down the street. The trudging women trudged, paused, came in and out of dark doors, talked to each other, to the men, to policemen, stared into shop windows, shouted at the children, laughed, stopped to caress them. All the faces, even those of the children, held a sweet or poisonous disenchantment which made their faces extraordinarily definite, as though they had been struck out of stone. The cab sped uptown, past men in front of barber shops, in front of barbecue joints, in front of bars; sped past side streets, long, dark, noisome, with gray houses leaning forward to cut out the sky; and in the shadow of these houses, children buzzed and boomed, as thick as flies on flypaper. Then they turned off the Avenue, west, crawled up a long, gray street. They had to crawl for the street was choked with unhurrying people and children kept darting out from between cars which were parked, for the length of the street, on either side. There were people on the stoops, people shouting out of windows, and young men peered indifferently into the slow-moving cab, their faces set ironically and their eyes unreadable.

James Baldwin, *Another Country* (New York: Dell, 1963), pp. 99-100.

The ghetto of Montreal has no real walls and no true dimensions. The walls are the habit of atavism and the dimensions are an illusion. But the ghetto exists all the same. The fathers say. "I work like this so it'll be better for the kids." A few of the fathers, the dissenters, do not crowd their days with work. They drink instead. But in the end it amounts to the same thing: in the end work, drink, or what have you, they are all trying to fill in the void.

Most of the Jews who live at the diminishing end of the ghetto, on streets named St. Urbain, St. Dominic, Rachel, and City Hall, work in textile or garment factories. Some are orthodox, others are communist. But all of them do their buying and their praying and their agitating and most of their sinning on St. Lawrence Boulevard, which is the aorta of the ghetto, reaching out in one direction towards Mount Royal, and past that (where it is no longer the ghetto) into the financial district and the factory slums, coming to a hard stop at the waterfront. In the other direction, northwards, St. Lawrence Boulevard approaches the fields at the city limits; where there is a rumour of grass and sun and quick spurious lovemaking.

All day long St. Lawrence Boulevard, or Main Street, is a frenzy of poor Jews, who gather there to buy groceries, furniture, clothing and meat. Most walls are plastered with fraying election bills, in Yiddish, French and English. The street reeks of garlic and quarrels and bill collectors: orange crates, stuffed full with garbage and decaying fruit, are piled slipshod in most alleys. Swift children gobble pilfered plums, slower cats prowl the fish market. After the water truck has passed, the odd dead rat can be seen floating down the gutter followed fast by rotten apples, cigar butts, chunks of horse manure and a terrifying zigzag of flies. Few stores go in for posh window displays. Instead, their windows are jammed full and pasted up with streamers that say ALL GOODS REDUCED or EVERYTHING MUST GO.

Every night St. Lawrence Boulevard is lit up like a neon cake and used-up men stumble out of a hundred different flophouses to mix with rabbinical students and pimps and Trotskyites and poolroom sharks. Hair tonic and water is consumed in back alleys. Swank whores sally at you out of the promised jubilee of all the penny arcades. Crap games flourish under lamp posts. You can take Rita the Polack up to the Liberty Rooms or you can listen to Panofsky speak on Tim Buck and The Worker. You can catch Bubbles Dawson doing her strip at the Roxie Follies. You can study Talmud at the Bnai Jacob Yeshiva, or you can look over the girls at the A.Z.A. Stag or Drag.

Conditions improve on the five streets between St. Lawrence Boulevard and Park Avenue. Most of the Jews who live on these streets market what is cut or pressed by their relations below St. Lawrence Boulevard. Others, the aspiring, own haberdashery stores, junk yards and basement zipper factories.

The employer and professional Jews own their own duplexes in Outremont, a mild residential area which begins above Park Avenue. They belong to the Freemasons, or, if they can't get into that organization, to the Knights of Pythias. Their sons study at McGill, where they are Zionists and opposed to anti-semitic fraternities. They shop on St. Lawrence Boulevard, where the Jews speak quaintly like the heroes of nightclub jokes.

Mordecai Richler, *Son of a Smaller Hero* (New York: Paperback Library Edition, 1965), pp. 13-14. (First published, 1958.)

It was in the stockyards that Jonas's friend had gotten rich, and so to Chicago the party was bound. They knew that one word, Chicago – and that was all they needed to know, at least until they reached the city. Then, tumbled out of the cars without ceremony, they were no better off than before; they stood staring down the vista of Dearborn 'Street, with its big black buildings towering in the distance, unable to realize that they had arrived, and why, when they said "Chicago," people no longer pointed in some direction, but instead looked perplexed, or laughed, or went on without paying any attention. . . . For the whole of the first day they wandered about in the midst of deafening confusion, utterly lost; and it was only at night that, cowering in the doorway of a house, they were finally discovered and taken by the policeman to the station. In the morning an interpreter was found, and they were taken and put upon a car, and taught a new word – "stockyards." Their delight at discovering that they were to get out of this adventure without losing another share of their possessions, it would not be possible to describe.

They sat and stared out of the window. They were on a street which seemed to run on for ever, mile after mile – thirty-four of them, if they had known it – and each side of it one uninterrupted row of wretched little two-storey frame buildings. Down every side street they could see it was the same – never a hill and never a hollow, but always the same endless vista of ugly and dirty little wooden buildings. Here and there would be a bridge crossing a filthy creek, with hard-baked mud shores and dingy sheds and docks along it; here and there would be a railroad crossing with a tangle of switches, and locomotives puffing, and rattling freight cars filing by; here and there would be a great factory, a dingy building with innumerable windows in it, and immense volumes of smoke pouring from the chimneys, darkening the air above and making filthy the earth beneath. But after each of these interruptions, the desolate procession would begin again – the procession of dreary little buildings.

A full hour before the party reached the city they had begun to note the perplexing changes in the atmosphere. It grew darker all the time, and upon the earth the grass seemed to grow less green. Every minute, as the train sped on, the colours of things became dingier; the fields were grown parched and yellow, the landscape hideous and bare. And along with the thickening smoke they began to notice another circumstance, a strange, pungent odour. They were not sure that it was unpleasant, this odour; some might have called it sickening, but their taste in odours was not developed, and they were only sure that it was curious. Now, sitting in the trolley car, they realized that they were on their way to the home of it – that they had travelled all the way from Lithuania to it. It was now no longer something far off and faint, that you caught in whiffs; you could literally taste it, as well as smell it – you could take hold of it, almost, and examine it at your leisure. They were divided in their opinions about it. It was an elemental odour, raw and crude; it was rich, almost rancid, sensual and strong. They were some who drank it in as if it were an intoxicant; there were others who put their hankerchiefs to their faces. The new emigrants were still tasting it, lost in wonder, when suddenly the car came to a halt, and the door was flung open, and a voice shouted – "Stockyards!"

Upton Sinclair, *The Jungle* (Harmondsworth: Penguin Books, 1965), pp. 30-31. (First published, 1906.)

1. From what point of view does Margaret Laurence look at the city? What aspects of city life seem to impress her? Does she seem favourably or unfavourably disposed towards city living?
2. Are you sympathetic to Margaret Laurence's view of the city? Do you think that a person born and brought up in a city might react differently from this writer?
3. Do you think the sculpture "Soft Manhattan" represents an unfavourable or favourable view of the city? In what respects would the sculpture differ from an aerial photograph of the same area?
4. What section of what city is being described in the reading from James Baldwin's *Another Country*? What is your evidence? What contrasts does the writer draw between the former and present character of this area? Why might it have changed in character?
5. What aspects of the area and its people does James Baldwin most emphasize? What impression does he communicate of the difficulties of life in the black ghettoes of American cities? Could this description fit any part of any Canadian city?
6. Locate the area described in *Son of a Smaller Hero* on a Montreal street map. From what point of view does the writer describe it? What characteristics of the area and its people does he emphasize? What seems to be his attitude towards them?
7. From the reading, what are the main activities of this area of Montreal? What social activities are carried on there in particular?
8. Compare this description with James Baldwin's description of Harlem. What are the main differences between the two areas?
9. From what part of Europe have the immigrants described in the passage from *The Jungle* come? Why did they choose to go to Chicago? What do they hope to achieve there? How did they probably travel from Europe to Chicago?
10. What is their first impression of Chicago? What kind of reception did they get? Why are they so confused at first?
11. Do you think the author's description of a late nineteenth century industrial town sounds authentic? What aspects of his description impress you most?
12. What is the immigrant's first impression of the Chicago stockyards? What goes on in the stockyards? What Canadian city was somewhat similar to Chicago in this regard?
13. Do you think the newcomers will enjoy a good life in their new home? What kind of environment have they been introduced to?

3.   Social Problems of the Contemporary City

The city exists because there are advantages in having activities and people concentrated in a relatively small area instead of inconveniently spread about. People benefit from living in cities because they find a range of job opportunities and social amenities in them. Thus many people find prosperity and happiness in the city. However, for many others the city is an unfulfilled promise. The poor and the racial minorities have quite a different view of urban life than do the middle class suburbanites. Long ignored, they are increasingly bringing their situation to the attention of the rest of the city, by one means or another. Not all of a city's social problems arise out of poverty or discrimination, but these are certainly among the most serious.

Poverty in Canada is real. Its numbers are not in the thousands, but the millions. There is more of it than our society can tolerate, more than our economy can afford, and far more than existing measures and efforts can cope with. Its persistence, at a time when the bulk of Canadians enjoy one of the highest standards of living in the world, is a disgrace.

What is poverty in Canada? Those who have seen it, felt it, experienced it – whether as its victims or as those trying to do something about it – can supply some telling descriptions. But one of the notable characteristics of poverty in modern times is that it is so located in both city and country, and often so disguised (it does not, for example, invariably go about in rags), that it can pass largely unnoticed by those in happier circumstances. An occasional glimpse from a car window; a television show or Saturday supplement article – these may be the only manifestations of it which touch many a middle-class consciousness. Yet the figures . . . show indisputably that it is there, almost everywhere in Canada, on a larger scale than most Canadians probably suspect.

One reason for poverty's partial invisibility is that the poor tend to be collectively inarticulate. Many of them lack the education and the organization to make themselves heard. For example, most of them are outside the ambit of the trade union movement. They have few spokesmen and groups to represent them and give voice to their needs.

Another difficulty is that it is all too easy, in Canada, to file poverty away under the heading of certain other long-standing national problems, and in this way to lose sight of it as a major problem in its own right. Thus many Canadians may assume that the problem of poverty is close to identical with the problem of low average incomes in the Atlantic Provinces and Eastern Quebec (especially their rural areas) and among the Indian and Eskimo populations. But this is an inaccurate impression. The *incidence* of poverty – the chance of a given person being poor –

is certainly much higher in the areas and among the groups just mentioned. But in terms of absolute numbers, between a third and a half of the total poverty in Canada is to be found among the white population of cities and towns west of Three Rivers. The resident of Montreal or Toronto need not travel far to see poverty first-hand; a subway fare will suffice. . . .

Economic Council of Canada, *Fifth Annual Review: The Challenge of Growth and Change,* (Ottawa, Queen's Printer, 1968).

American cities could become nightmares of rape, robbery and murder unless conditions that lead to crime are checked soon, a presidential commission warned.

If this happened, a report released by the national commission on the causes and prevention of violence said, the cities would soon degenerate into "defensive, fearful societies."

"The report said powerful social forces in the slums and black ghettos, including the rising demands of minority groups, are threatening to explode.

It said violent crime in the cities is greatest among youths aged 15 to 24 and stemmed disproportionately from the black ghetto slums.

But commission chairman Milton Eisenhower said this does not mean there is a correlation between race and crime.

"The correlation," he said, "is poverty with crime."

The commission said, as it has done before, that an improved system of criminal justice is required to contain the growth of violent crime. Law-enforcement agencies also needed strengthening.

"But only progress toward urban reconstruction can reduce the strength of the crime-causing forces in the inner city and thus reverse the direction of present crime trends," it commented.

The report painted the following grim picture, already largely true, of how big cities might look in a few more years:

Central business districts in the heart of the city, surrounded by areas of accelerating deterioration, will be partially protected by large numbers of people shopping or working in commercial buildings during daytime hours, plus a substantial police presence, and will be largely deserted except for police patrols during night hours.

High-rise apartment buildings and residential compounds, protected by private guards and security devices, will be fortified cells for upper middle- and high-income populations living at prime locations in the city.

Lacking a sharp change in federal and state policies, ownership of guns will be almost universal in the suburbs. Homes will be fortified by an array of devices from window grills to electronic surveillance equipment.

High-speed, patrolled highways will be sanitized corridors connecting safe areas, and private cars, taxis and commercial vehicles will be routinely equipped with unbreakable glass, light armor and other security features. Armed guards will "ride shot-gun" on all forms of public transportation.

From Reuters News Agency Report of the "President's Commission on Violence" (Eisenhower Commission), reported in the *Vancouver Sun* (November, 1969).

Prime Minister Pierre Trudeau was talking to a group of Queen's University students last November when he said, "I am less worried about what is over the Berlin Wall than about what might happen in Chicago or in New York or in our great cities in Canada." No one seemed to be listening. But last week Canada learned what he meant. The television scenes of sniper fire, shattered storefronts and armed soldiers patrolling the streets were all a familiar part of the newsreels of the sixties. The shock this time was that they came not via the U.S. networks, but live from Montreal. For the first time in any major Canadian urban center, the police and fire departments walked off their jobs in a wildcat strike, leaving a frightened city at the mercy of its own worst elements for 16 hours. The result was a night of lawlessness in the country's largest metropolis that caused one death, an estimated $2,350,000 in damage and, by the time it ended, the Quebec provincial police and the army had been called in.

It seems to be Montreal's fate to alter in climacteric ways the image that Canadians have of themselves and their country. Just two years ago Montreal did so in a brilliantly creative fashion with the sophisticated elegance of Expo 67. Last week the image was distressingly different. The city's day without the law sent a tremor across the land, effectively dispelling the comfortable notion that it can't happen here. As urban riots go, the city's violence was a relatively lesser quake on the North American scale. And the disorders clearly owed much to particular tensions that Montreal shares with no other Canadian city. Yet for all that, the nightmare reflected a breakdown of old constraints; it suggested that Canadian urban centers can no longer consider themselves immune from the social unrest that has swept other countries.

Time (October 17, 1969).

14. Does the Economic Council feel poverty is a major problem in Canada? Why is it sometimes overlooked? In which parts of Canada are most of the poor to be found?

15. What groups make up "the urban poor"? What can be done to help these groups? What is being done now? Is it adequate?

16. According to the news report, what is the basis of the growth of violent crime in the United States? Do you think that this is an adequate explanation?

17. Why should violent crime be highest among young, black ghetto dwellers in the United States? Who are the probable victims of this crime? Is the situation similar in Canada?

18. What remedies are proposed by the Presidential Commission to hold down the crime wave? Do you think that these will be adequate?

19. If the crime wave is not halted, what does the report suggest will be the consequences for the city of the future? Is Canada likely to follow this pattern?
20. What insight into the conditions that help create urban violence does the passage from *Another Country,* quoted earlier, provide?
21. What event is being referred to in the excerpt from *Time* magazine? Do you agree that this incident demonstrates that Canadian cities are as prone to violence as American cities?

4.   Ear, Nose, and Eye Pollution

With the growth of industry many new problems of urban living have appeared. The economic prosperity which creates jobs often seems to create the things which make life unpleasant and as they grow in size, cities also seem to become dirtier, smellier, noisier, and uglier. In recent times the problems of air and water pollution have become so pressing that some have seriously asked whether urban man can survive into the twenty-first century. Though by no means as dangerous, the problems of noise and ugliness are making cities less attractive as places to live. These are some more of the social costs that can offset the economic benefits of living in cities.

> WELCOME SULPHUR DIOXIDE
> HELLO CARBON MONOXIDE
> THE AIR THE AIR
> IS EVERYWHERE
> BREATHE DEEP
> WHILE YOU SLEEP
> BREATHE DEEP
> Gerome Ragni and James Rado, *Hair*

The advanced nations of the world are deeply preoccupied with preserving habitable conditions in their cities. The shanty towns are growing up with none of the services which are just enabling European and American cities to hold their own.

Yet it has been estimated that urban growth in undeveloped regions is now going ahead far faster than in developed regions. Between 1920 and the end of this century, the urban population of the developed countries is expected to quadruple; the urban population of undeveloped countries will multiply 20 times, so that nearly twice as many people will be town dwellers in poor regions as in rich.

The rich are now discovering the enormous overheads of

city living, the vast investment and maintenance involved in keeping the great conurbations functioning at all (and even then, there is horrible decay in the centre of places like Chicago).

There seems little prospect that the poor regions will be able to invest even a fraction of what will be needed to prevent the development of tropical slums which will make Chicago's ghettos seem like a garden of Eden.

To appreciate the problems, it helps to look in more detail at one or two of the urban problems of advanced countries. Take the generation of waste, an activity pioneered with special energy in the United States which shows the shape of things to come.

Each American citizen produces some three-quarters of a ton of solid refuse per year. Los Angeles alone dumps 12 million cubic yards of refuse each year into dumps and landfills.

The wonders of the modern packaging industry mean that a growing proportion of this refuse is indestructible – 48 billion aluminium cans are discarded annually, 28 billion long-lived jars and bottles, and uncounted plastic containers and wrappings. If they are incinerated, there is an air-pollution problem.

Giant car-dumps are a familiar feature of the landscape, and have prompted the development of colossal plants which grind up old cars into small bits.

Mining companies are said to be eyeing certain American scrapheaps as a potentially richer source of minerals than those provided by nature.

Even more formidable is the United States sewage industry, which by the year 2000 will be dealing with almost 37 billion gallons of municipal sewage a day, or about 132 gallons per person per day, to which are added 1.3 billion gallons a day of industrial effluent.

The latest sewage problem comes from the urbanization of farming. Instead of depositing their manure as precious fertilizer on fields, animals on factory farms have the equivalent of running water and flushing toilets.

The result is vast quantities of odorous slurry, which is becoming a major disposal problem. Thus we have the weird spectacle of farmers buying in subsidized fertilizer from the chemical industry, and operating a subsidized farming system which may need more subsidies to dispose of the unsubsidized fertilizer produced free by the animals.

The rivers are not our only sinks. We use the air as well. It is estimated that into the air over the United States there are dumped annually 65 million tons of carbon monoxide, 23 million tons of sulphur compounds, 15 million tons of acrid substances, 12 million tons of dust, 8 million tons of acrid nitrogen compounds, and 2 million tons of other gases and vapours.

It is predicted that even with severe control, these amounts will more than double by the end of the century.

John Davy, "Poison Perils Our Planet," *Vancouver Sun,* November 30, 1968 (rep. from *London Observer*).

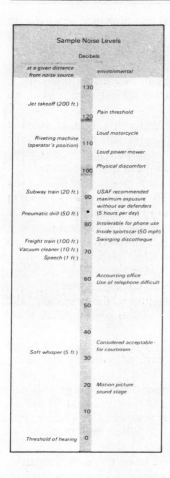

Fig. 8-2 Sample Noise Levels

Noise levels in our cities and on our highways are today high enough to constitute a major physical and mental health hazard. Art Seidenbaum stated the case succinctly earlier this year in his Los Angeles Times column: "The day of the decibels is upon us and aural air pollution has become one of the issues of survival."

Dr. Vern O. Knudsen, former chancellor of the University of California at Los Angeles and a distinguished physicist who has spent 40 years studying sound, describes noise as

> . . . . one of the waste products of the 20th century – as unwanted and unnecessary as smog, polluted water or littered streets. It is one of the chief drawbacks to the enjoyment of modern urban living.

Noise impairs hearing, impedes convalescence, hinders concentrated mental effort, interferes with relaxation and sleep ("If it did nothing else but interfere with sleep, noise would be a menace to good health," says Dr. Knudsen), and perhaps most

Fig. 8-3 Urban Clutter

important, causes stress and nervousness and thus the troubles that are associated with tension – irritability, insomnia, accident proneness, and cardiovascular diseases.

. . . No one tolerates painful light intensities willingly. As light intensity increases, the pupil first contracts automatically and then the eyes squint and close. However, the ear, lacking a pupil and an earlid, has to take whatever the environment has to offer, at least up to the level where one defensively closes his ears with his fingers.

Until the beginning of the Industrial Revolution, the loudest noises in civilization were the ringing of a blacksmith's anvil, the blare of a trumpet and the screeching of an angered fishwife. But with the advent of the steam engine, then the internal combustion engine and now the jet, the Noise Age has become a strident reality. It is generally accepted that community sound levels have increased one decibel a year for the last 30 years, and there is no end in sight. Dr. Knudsen commented on our prospects: "Noise, like smog, is a slow agent of death. If it continues to increase for the next 30 years as it had for the past 30 it could become lethal."

William Bronson, "Ear Pollution," *Cry California*, II, No. 4 (Fall, 1967), 28-30.

---

22. In the article from the *Vancouver Sun*, what is meant by: "the enormous overheads of city living," "great conurbations," "Chicago's ghettos," and "industrial effluent." What problems are referred to in this reading? Why are they considered to be most intense in urban areas, and especially in the urban areas of the undeveloped regions.

23. What particular sources of pollution does the writer mention? What others can you think of? Which could be regarded as examples of air or water pollution?

24. What solutions might be proposed to each of the particular problems mentioned and what might stand in the way of their being put into practice.

25. Which of the sounds mentioned in Figure 8-2 might be commonly heard in the city streets? Which of these are above the level of physical discomfort?

26. According to Dr. Knudsen, why are the problems mentioned in the third reading serious?

27. What shortcomings, if any, would you suggest might be found in the scenes shown in Figure 8-3? What improvements would you introduce to make it conform more with your own taste?

5.   Suburbs and Satellites

The English town planner Sir Ebenezer Howard compared the town and the country to two opposing magnets each exerting a force attracting population. He proposed as a solution to the uncontrolled sprawl of the industrial cities of his era the construction of self contained Garden Cities which would combine the advantages of town and country. With the growth in car ownership it is now possible for large numbers of people to flee the city and build homes in the country, but the suburbs created in the process soon develop many of the disadvantages of the city itself. As an alternative to haphazard suburban growth many countries have built satellite cities like those proposed by Howard.

The Town magnet, it will be seen, offers, as compared with the Country magnet, the advantages of high wages, opportunities for employment, tempting prospects of advancement, but these are largely counterbalanced by high rents and prices. Its social opportunities and its places of amusement are very alluring, but excessive hours of toil, distance from work, and the "isolation of crowds" tend greatly to reduce the value of these good things. The well-lit streets are a great attraction, especially in winter, but the sunlight is being more and more shut out, while the air is so vitiated that the fine public buildings, like the sparrows, rapidly become covered with soot, and the very statues are in despair. Palatial edifices and fearful slums are the strange, complementary features of modern cities.

The Country magnet declares herself to be the source of all beauty and wealth; but the Town magnet mockingly reminds her that she is very dull for lack of society, and very sparing of her gifts for lack of capital. There are in the country beautiful vistas, lordly parks, violet-scented woods, fresh air, sounds of rippling water; but too often one sees those threatening words, "Trespassers will be prosecuted." Rents, if estimated by the acre, are certainly low, but such low rents are the natural fruit of low wages rather than a cause of substantial comfort; while long hours and lack of amusements forbid the bright sunshine and the pure air to gladden the hearts of the people. The one industry, agriculture, suffers frequently from excessive rainfalls; but this wondrous harvest of the clouds is seldom properly ingathered, so that, in times of drought, there is frequently, even for drinking purposes, a most insufficient supply. Even the natural healthfulness of the country is largely lost for lack of proper drainage and other sanitary conditions, while, in parts almost deserted by the people, the few who remain are yet frequently huddled together as if in rivalry with the slums of our cities.

Ebenezer Howard, *Garden Cities of Tomorrow* (London: Faber & Faber, 1946), p. 47. (First published, 1902.)

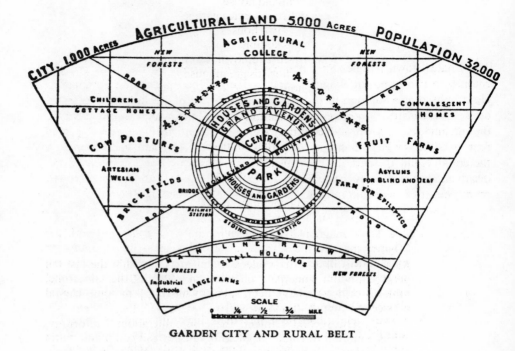

GARDEN CITY AND RURAL BELT

Fig. 8-4 Ebenezer Howard's proposed Garden City

Though the complaints and sorrows of the suburbs appear in many different versions, they can be grouped under three main titles: the Lament about Muddle, the Lament about Uniformity, and the Lament about What Isn't There.

You don't have to go very far to find a good example of the suburban city's muddle and confusion. Not five minutes' distance from where these words are written is a suburban street in the capital city of Canada that displays the tangled confusion typical of suburbia. It does not flatter the distinguished Prime Minister whose name it bears. Along one side of the street, with its counterpart on the other, in a distance of just one mile, are those buildings with a few empty lots interspersed:

two gas stations
a builders' supply plant
a house
a gas station
a house
a gas station
two small restaurants

a small apartment house
an old house
a delivery service garage
two houses
a gas station
a furniture removal warehouse
a florist's greenhouse
a house
a restaurant
a gas station
a grocery store
a barber shop
a restaurant
a large high school
a house
an elementary school
six houses
a licensed hotel

Most of this ill-assorted collection has arrived within the last ten years, an odd commentary on a city in which, at the same time, millions of dollars have been spent to make the national capital a place of beauty and reason. . . .

. . . The second Lament, the complaint about Uniformity, raises a more intractable problem because it is a complaint about the very thing that everyone claims to want. We staged a technological and social revolution, we got cars and home-financing, so that everyone could take the long road out to the suburbs. This was to be a way of life offering the greatest opportunity for the free expression of the individual. And here at the end of the road is the modern suburb with its stereotyped houses and the threat of stereotyped behaviour. It turns out that life in the suburbs is not such a privilege after all. Almost everyone else lives there too. There are more of us all the time and there are fewer differences between us. The less privileged families live in 1,000 sq. ft. bungalows, the majority live in 1,200 sq. ft. houses, and the really privileged live in 1,400 sq. ft. Only 200 square feet and a difference of a few inches in the lengths of our cars separate the sheep from the goats. The flight to the suburbs has taken us to a monotonous, standardized environment where everyone has much the same amount of money to do much the same things in the same ways. This is the complaint.

. . . The final Lament completes the triad: the Lament about What Isn't There, the expression of a shadowy intuition that Something is Missing. This lament is often cast in the abstract and emotional language of frustration. "There's no There there." People say there's "nothing to identify with" – whatever that may mean. The suburbs are just more of the same thing. Middle distances and middle incomes and middling results. No destination and nothing unexpected around the corner. Nothing very big and nothing very beautiful. The shopping centre's the most

pronounced place; you've been there before and you come back
bearing the same brown paper bag, for you're a consumer, average
and typical. It's a relief to go downtown because it's large enough
to lose yourself in. There are big buildings and even some beautiful buildings and you can look up and see the sky behind their
summits. There are long distances and short distances as well as
middle distances. They say downtown is now a place for the very
rich and the very poor, a place of extremes, of excellence and of
tragedy. In the open landscape of the countryside there are also
great contrasts. You can see a long way and place yourself under
the arch of the firmament. And on the ground are small things
like flowers and pebbles. But in the suburbs there are no extremes.

Humphrey Carver, *Cities in the Suburbs* (Toronto: University of Toronto
Press, 1962), pp. 12-13, 15, 18.

A CITY OF BEAUTIFUL HOMES . . .
Homes in Bramalea are designed for the middle and upper-middle
incomes and the number of designs in each price range is extensive. Lots are spacious, allowing for abundant lawn and shrubs
and, wherever possible, existing trees and natural wooded areas
have been retained and are incorporated into each developed
area. A series of crescents, winding roads, boulevards, along with
the trees, flowers and shrubs makes for one beautiful scene after
another throughout Bramalea.

A FAMILY CITY . . .
Bramalea has all the advantages of city as well as country living,
but not the problems of either. There is no traffic congestion,
crowding and pollution, as in densely populated areas. An abund-
ance of pure air to breathe, open fields, lush greenbelt, plenty of
social and recreational activities and an industrial segment to
provide self-sufficiency – that's what makes Bramalea an ideal
suburban city for families.

Brochure from Bramalea Consolidated Developments Ltd.

Little boxes on the hillside,
Little boxes made of ticky tacky,
Little boxes on the hillside,
Little boxes all the same.
There's a green one, and a pink one,
And a blue one and a yellow one,
And they're all made out of ticky tacky,
And they all look just the same.

And the people in the houses
All went to the university,
Where they were put in boxes
And they came out all the same,

And there's doctors and lawyers,
And business executives,
And they're all made out of ticky tacky,
And they all look just the same.

And they all play on the golf course
And drink their martinis dry,
And they all have pretty children
And the children go to school,
And the children go to summer camp
And then to the university,
Where they are put in boxes
And they come out all the same.

And the boys go into business
And marry and raise a family,
In boxes made of ticky tacky
And they all look just the same.
There's a green one, and a pink one,
And a blue one and a yellow one,
And they're all made out of ticky tacky,
And they all look just the same.

Malvina Reynolds

28. What did Ebenezer Howard see as the main advantages and disadvantages of the town and the country. How did he propose to combine them in the Garden City shown diagrammatically in Figure 8-4?

29. In the excerpt from Humphrey Carver's *Cities in the Suburbs,* the writer criticizes the suburbs on three counts. What are they and what explanation would you put forward for their existence? How do the suburbs as pictured by Carver differ from the ideal Garden City shown in Howard's diagram?

30. Do the excerpts from the brochure issued by the developers of Bramalea suggest that this particular satellite town answers the criticisms of the suburbs levelled by Carver? If so, to what degree? To what extent does Bramalea (described also on p. 122) come close to the ideal expressed by Howard? Do you think that it is intended to do so? Or that it should?

31. Do you feel that the criticism suggested in the song is a justified one?

6. Urban Prospects

To many the prospects of the city in the latter part of the twentieth century seem grim indeed. While U Thant draws attention to the plight of cities throughout the world and the challenge they present for the future, the distinguished

American urban critic Lewis Mumford regrets their loss of the human dimension. Solutions of many kind have been put forward to the problems presented by a greatly expanding urban population. Some think technical solutions are possible and call for the introduction of completely different kinds of urban form, like the revolutionary projections of Buckminster Fuller, inventor of the geodesic dome and designer of the United States pavilion at Expo 67. Others, like the famous historian Arnold Toynbee, suggest that man can only continue to live in cities through a turning inward to values of the spirit.

Most Americans think they know what is meant by "the urban crisis." To many, it means Watts in Los Angeles, the Hough section of Cleveland, Harlem in New York – in short, race riots, poverty, slums. To others, the urban crisis is manifest daily in clogged freeways, rising land costs, and inadequate parks, plus a persistent dissatisfaction with urban life. But how many Americans think of the appalling squalor of the favelas of Rio de Janeiro, the bidonvilles of Algiers, the vecindades of Mexico City, or the nocturnal streets, littered with sleeping bodies, of Calcutta? There, the urban crisis is compounded by the lack of shelter, food, jobs and, above all, hope.

Last week Secretary General U Thant reported to the Economic and Social Council of the United Nations that the city – everywhere in the world – is a failure. For example, the U.N. proposed that the developing nations build at least ten units of housing per 1,000 people annually. In many countries only two units per 1,000 people have actually been constructed.

The challenge in the two decades ahead, the report went on, is to "double the houses, power systems, sanitation, schools, transport, in fact the whole complex pattern of urban living created over several centuries." Can this goal be accomplished? The record in both rich and poor nations is discouraging, though there are a few bright examples. Through high-level planning, Russia, Britain, Venezuela and India have encouraged the rise of small cities to decentralize population. France and Bulgaria fostered new, strategically located regional centers. Switzerland and The Netherlands have attempted with some success to balance growth between cities and rural towns.

Still, population is relentlessly exploding in what the report terms "unexploding economies." In the next decade, 18 Latin American cities will probably contain 1,000,000 or more inhabitants each, whether the nations are prepared for the flood of humanity or not. Bombay and Calcutta might swell to 20 million or even 30 million residents by the end of the century.

To cope with the pressure of new people, U Thant said, advance planning for cities is imperative. At least 5% of national income should be allocated to housing and urban development. Local construction industries should quickly be strengthened, savings institutions established, and research centers created to study specific urban problems. Beyond the particular effort of every nation, there must be international cooperation. The richer nations should aid developing nations with at least $1 billion in seed money annually. Nations should also get together to set up training centers for personnel and to pool social and technical information.

The report provides a unique global view of a depressing, but neglected and far-reaching subject. We are all in the same boat, it says in effect, and the boat is foundering. It also stitches together various urban experiments from nations of differing political persuasions to form a patchwork solution. Most important, U Thant's report offers, along with extremely pessimistic statistics about the present, an infectious optimism about the future – if nations can learn to cooperate.

Time (September 12, 1969).

As one moves away from the center, the urban growth becomes ever more aimless and discontinuous, more diffuse and un-focussed, except where some surviving town has left the original imprint of a more orderly life. Old neighbourhoods and precincts. the social cells of the city, still maintaining some measure of the village pattern, become vestigial. No human eye can take in this metropolitan mass at a glance. No single gathering place except the totality of its streets can hold all its citizens. No human mind can comprehend more than a fragment of the complex and minutely specialized activities of its citizens. The loss of form, the loss of autonomy, the constant frustration and harassment of daily activities, to say nothing of gigantic breakdowns and stop-pages – all these become normal attributes of the metropolitan regime. There is a special name for power when it is concentrated on such a scale: it is called impotence.

The giantism of the metropolis is not the result of techno-logical progress alone. Contrary to popular belief, the growth of great cities preceded the decisive technical advances of the last two centuries. But the metropolitan phase became universal only when the technical means of congestion had become adequate – and their use profitable to those who manufactured or employed them. The modern metropolis is, rather, an outstanding example of a peculiar cultural lag within the realm of technics itself: namely, the continuation by highly advanced technical means of the obsolete forms and ends of a socially retarded civilization. The machines and utilities that would lend themselves to decen-tralization in a life-centered order, here become either a means to increased congestion or afford some slight temporary palliation – at a price.

The form of the metropolis, then, is its formlessness, even as its aim is its own aimless expansion. Those who work within the ideological limits of this regime have only a quantitative concep-tion of improvement: they seek to make its buildings higher, its streets broader, its parking lots more ample: they would multiply bridges, highways, tunnels, making it ever easier to get in and out of the city, but constricting the amount of space available within the city for any other purposes than transportation itself. Frank Lloyd Wright's project for a skyscraper a mile high was the ultimate reduction to absurdity of this whole theory of city development. The ultimate form of such a city would be an acre of building to a square mile of expressways and parking lots. In many areas this is rapidly approaching fulfillment.

Lewis Mumford, *The City in History* (New York: Harcourt, Brace and World, 1961), pp. 543-4.

The new Queen Elizabeth is a luxuriously comfortable abode either at sea or in port. She is a mobile city. She is shaped to get passengers across oceans in a hurry. If such floating cities didn't have to speed, they might have an efficiently symmetrical shape. It is eminently feasible and economical to develop floatable organic cities of immense size. To visualize the various design-controlling conditions under which such cities could be constructed, imagine pinching a camera tripod's legs together, taking hold of the bottom of the tripod in one hand and trying to hold it vertically on the top of an automobile going 70 miles an hour, over rough terrain. As you opened the legs of the tripod – each time you spread them – the tripod would get steadier and steadier. This is the stabilizing effect obtained when tension stays are rigged from top to bottom on three sides of a mast, as with radio towers. It is equally effective to have the legs spread outwardly, as in the Eiffel Tower. When the three legs are spread apart so that the length of the edges of their base triangle equals the length of each of the legs themselves, the tripod attains its maximum stability. This conformation is that of the regular, or equilateral, tetrahedron. As the tripod's legs go farther apart than the regular tetrahedron, its top can support less and less load. Thus we learn that the most stable structure is the regular, equiedged tetrahedron.

Following this design science clue, we find that a tetrahedral city to house 1,000,000 people is both technologically and economically feasible. Such a hollow tetrahedral city can be constructed with each of its 300,000 families having terraced "outside" apartments of 2,000 square feet each. The terraces would permit the storage of mobile trailers, houseboats and other mobile homes, leaving an additional 1,000 square feet for a garden. The living units would be weatherproofed and would require no additional "walls," or external skins, to be fastened onto the tetrahedral city. Such a city would consist of an open-truss-framework "structural mountain," whose sides are covered with parked mobile homes. At night, it would be ablaze with light, as are the great petroleum refineries. All of the organic machinery necessary to its operation would be housed behind the three principal "walls" of the tetrahedron.

Tetrahedrons are also geometrically unique in that they grow symmetrically by additions to any one of their faces. Tetrahedral cities may start with 1,000 occupants and grow to hold millions

Fig. 8-5 The U.S. Pavilion at Expo 67

without changing their over-all shape and always providing each family with 2,000 square feet of floor space. Such a city would be so structurally efficient and therefore so relatively light that, together with its foundation – of hollow sections of reinforced concrete – it could float. The model floating city would measure two miles to an edge. Its foundation would be 200 feet or more in depth and several hundred feet wide. On land, the structure could float in a three-sided moat, which would make the whole city earthquakeproof. Or the structure could be floated out into the ocean to any point and anchored. The depth of its foundation would go below the turbulent level of the seas, so that it would be, in effect, a floating triangular atoll. Its two-mile base, would provide landing strips for jet airplanes. Its interior two-mile harbour would provide refuge for the largest ocean vessels.

Buckminster Fuller, "The City of the Future," *Playboy* (July, 1968), p. 166.

City walls were for defence against dangers that were external and tangible. The enemies that had to be kept out were wild beasts or, if human beings, they were barbarians or aliens. In Megalopolis, the need for defence is going to be more urgent than it ever was in Tiryns or in Troy, but the enemy now will be internal and the danger will be psychological. Man is paying for having overcome external dangers by becoming a still greater danger to himself. He is the victim of his triumphant science, technology and organization. Technology has inflated the material setting of human life to an inhuman scale. Man is being dwarfed by his apparatus and stifled by his numbers, and this heavy physical pressure on the individual is inflicting a severe psychic distress. The problem of defence in Megalopolis is the problem of how to rehumanize life when it has to be lived in a man-made infinity of people, buildings and streets. Megalopolis is going to encompass the earth. In material terms there is going to be no escape from it. Liberation from it will have to be sought by turning inwards from the physical world to the psyche and to the ultimate spiritual presence that is "the dweller in the innermost" besides being the creator and sustainer of the universe. This way of salvation would have been less difficult for modern Western man's medieval forebears to take than it is for their present-day descendants; for, since the beginning of the modern age of Western history, Western man has been investing his efforts and his treasure in the mastery of his material environment. Now that his achievement of this mastery is forcing him back upon himself in self-defence against the dehumanized world that his technology has conjured up, he finds himself at a loss; and the non-Western majority of the human race is going to fall into the same straits as it becomes more and more deeply implicated in the "extrovert" modern Western way of life. Megalopolis is going to swallow up human beings of all cultures, religions and races; for all of us, the problem of having to live in Megalopolis will have to be solved in spiritual terms. The town-planner cannot do our spiritual work for us; but perhaps he can help by mitigating the pressure of the physical environment. Perhaps he can articulate the endless chaos of buildings and crowds into human-sized quarters within which we can, once again, enter into personal relations with a limited circle of neighbours. Perhaps he can plan these quarters so that we can go about our daily business on foot, and our children can come and go between home and school without being made to risk death through being compelled to cross speedways infested with high-powered mechanized traffic. In fact, we need town-planners with the human imagination and the professional skill to re-create Weimars[1] and Cranfords[2] for us as cities of refuge in Megalopolis's shapeless wilderness. This was the solution which was suggested, half playfully, by Chesterton[3] in *The Napoleon of Notting Hill* in the early years of the twentieth century, when the roar of the

[1]A German city noted in the early nineteenth century for its elegant planning.
[2]An English market town, described in the novel *Cranford* by Mrs. Gaskell.
[3]G. K. Chesterton, the English novelist (1872-1936).

coming Megalopolis was already audible to a sensitive soul's inner ear.

Spiritual defences for life in Megalopolis can be found, and they can be as effective as the physical defences of Jericho were till Joshua's trumpets sounded, and as those of Troy were till its walls were wantonly breached to make an entry for the wooden horse. Change is of the essence of life. We have exposed ourselves to a revolutionary agency of change in learning, all too well, how to accelerate the progress of technology; and any response to a challenge that we may make today is hardly likely to hold good for the next two thousand million years. In any case, defences – even when successful – are never enough, and this is also true of defences against life in Megalopolis. Aristotle maintains that cities were brought into existence originally to make life possible, but that the ultimate purpose of them is to make life worth living. This dictum reads ironically today, when Megalopolis is the city in which we are going to have to live. Yet Aristotle is surely right. Mere existence on the defensive cannot satisfy human beings; so we have to make life worth living, even in Megalopolis, and this means making spiritual room, in Megalopolis, for the inner life of human feelings, ideas, ideals and purposes. Since this field of life is a spiritual one, each human soul has to find salvation in it for himself. But, here again, the town-planner, if he has the imagination and the skill, can help the citizens of Megalopolis to win their spiritual battle. He can help by providing them, in inspiring visible forms, with material symbols of these invisible spiritual treasures.

Arnold Toynbee, *Cities of Destiny* (New York: McGraw Hill, 1967), pp. 27-8.

---

32. Why does the article from *Time* suggest that the understanding which most Americans have of "the urban crisis" might be an inadequate one?
33. What steps have the countries cited in the article taken as an attempt to control the population growth of large urban centres? What are the advantages, or disadvantages, of the solutions mentioned?
34. What steps did U Thant suggest should be taken to deal with urban problems?
35. To what problems of urbanization does Lewis Mumford draw attention? In what ways are these problems different from those reported by U Thant?
36. Do you regard Buckminster Fuller's design for a city of the future a satisfactory solution to the problems mentioned either by U Thant or Lewis Mumford?
37. What does Arnold Toynbee suggest is the role of the planner? What other factor does he consider essential to a continued existence in Megalopolis?
38. Do you agree with Aristotle's dictum that the ultimate purpose of cities is "to make life worth living"?

References

The following books and articles have been drawn upon in the preparation of this text. Many of the ideas introduced here are discussed much more thoroughly in these original works.

Alexander, J. W., "The Basic-Nonbasic Concept of Urban Economic Function," *Economic Geography,* 30 (1954), pp. 246-61.

Berry, B., *Commercial Structure and Commercial Blight,* University of Chicago, Department of Geography, Research Paper No. 85, 1963.

Buttimer, A., "Social Space in Interdisciplinary Perspective," *Geographical Review,* Vol. 59 (1969), p. 417.

Carver, H., *Cities in the Suburbs,* Toronto, University of Toronto Press, 1962.

Christaller, Walter, *The Central Places of Southern Germany,* trs. by Carlisle W. Baskin, Englewood Cliffs, N.J., Prentice-Hall Inc., 1966.

Dickinson, R., *City and Region,* New York, Humanities Press, 1964.

Gottman, Jean, *Megalopolis,* Cambridge, Mass., M.I.T. Press, 1961.

Jones, E., *Towns and Cities,* London, Eng., Oxford University Press, 1965.

Maxwell, J., "The Functional Structure of Canadian Cities," *Geographical Bulletin,* Vol. 7 (1965), p. 79.

Mumford, L., *The City in History,* New York, Harcourt, Brace and World, 1961.

Murdie, R., *A Factorial Ecology of Metropolitan Toronto 1951-1961,* University of Chicago, Department of Geography, Research Paper No. 116, 1969.

Robinson, I., *New Industrial Towns on Canada's Resource Frontier,* University of Chicago, Department of Geography, Research Paper No. 73, 1963.

Simmons, J., "Changing Residence in the City: A Review of Intra-Urban Mobility," *Geographical Review,* Vol. 58 (1968), p. 622.

Simmons, J., and Simmons, R., *Urban Canada,* Toronto, Copp Clark, 1969.

Smailes, A., *The Geography of Towns,* London, Eng., Hutchinson, 1960.

Stone, L., *Urban Development in Canada,* Ottawa, Queen's Printer, 1968.

Acknowledgements

We should like to acknowledge the assistance given by the following individuals and groups in the preparation of this text.

For permission to reproduce or adapt photographs, tables, and maps:

L. Bell and United Community Services of the Greater Vancouver Area for Figs. 6-1, 6-3, 6-4, 6-7, 6-10, reproduced from L. Bell, *Metropolitan Vancouver: An Overview for Social Planners* (1965).

B. Berry and Department of Geography, University of Chicago, for Table 5-1, from data appearing in B. Berry, *Commercial Structure and Commercial Blight,* University of Chicago, Department of Geography, Research Paper No. 85 (1965).

Bramalea Consolidated Developments for Fig. 7-3 and excerpts from brochure copy.

Brookings Institute and W. Owen for Table 7-4 and related data, reproduced by permission of the original publisher, Brookings Inst., from W. Owen, *Metropolitan Transportation Problems* (New York: Anchor, 1966). ©copyright Brookings Institute.

The Editor of *Canadian Mining and Metallurgical Magazine* for Figs. 2-12 and 2-13, from "Symposium on the Thompson Operation of Inco," *Canadian Mining and Metallurgical Magazine* (November, 1964).

Canadian National Railways for Fig. 1-3.

Department of Energy, Mines, and Resources for Figs. 2-5, 4-7, and 5-2.

Editor of the *Geographical Bulletin* and J. Maxwell for Fig. 3-4, from J. Maxwell, "Functional Classification of Canadian Cities," *Geographical Bulletin* (1965).

Editor of the *Geographical Review* and J. Simmons for Table 6-2, from J. Simmons, "Changing Residences in the City: A Review of Intra-Urban Mobility," *Geographical Review* (1968), p. 622.

Government of Saskatchewan, Department of Industry and Commerce, for data in Table 3-2.

Halifax Port Commission for Fig. 5-3.

International Nickel Company for Fig. 2-11.

Institute of Public Administration of Canada and G. Hodge for Table 3-3, from G. Hodge, "Urban Systems and Regional Policy," *Canadian Public Administration,* Vol. 9 (1966).

Kingston *Whig-Standard* and Mrs. J. Wolforth for Fig. 4-12.

Mrs. A. McAfee for Fig. 6-13, reproduced from "Residence on the margin of the C.B.D.," M.A. thesis, Department of Geography, University of British Columbia, 1967.

C. Mayhew and United Community Services of the Greater Vancouver Area for Fig. 5-4, from C. Mayhew, *Local Area Atlas of Vancouver* (1967).

Metropolitan Toronto Planning Board for Figs. 7-8, 7-10, and 7-12.

D. Montgomery for Figs. 5-8 and 5-10, from "Internal Structure of Urban Arterial Business Ribbons," M.A. thesis, Department of Geography, University of British Columbia, 1967.

National Film Board for Figs. 2-2, 2-8, 3-3, 5-1, 6-6B, 7-6, 7-11, 7-13, 8-3B, and 8-5.

National Harbours Board for Fig. 4-2.

Nova Scotia Information Service for Fig. 1-7.

Queen's Printer and L. Stone for Tables 1-1, 3-6, and Figs. 1-2, 6-5, from L. Stone, *Urban Canada* (Ottawa, 1968), reproduced with the permission of Information Canada.

Safeway (Canada) Ltd., for Fig. 4-4.

Steel Company of Canada for Fig. 2-10.

Tantalus Research Limited and J. Wolforth for Figs. 4-1 and 6-14, from J. Wolforth, *Residential Location and the Place of Work* (Vancouver, 1964).

Toronto *Globe and Mail* for Figs. 7-7 and 7-9.

Toronto Transit Commission for Fig. 1-5.

University of British Columbia, Special Collections, for Figs. 2-1, 2-4, 2-6, 2-7, and 2-9.

University of Toronto Press for permission to adapt Fig. 7-4 from a map appearing in the *Economic Atlas of Ontario* (1969).

Vancouver Art Gallery for Fig. 8-1.

Vancouver Sun for Fig. 5-5.

Western Pacific Projects Ltd. for Figs. 5-6 and 5-7.

For permission to reprint copyrighted material:

Barnes and Noble, for excerpts from W. L. Grant (ed.), *Voyages of Samuel de Champlain 1604-1618* (New York, 1907), pp. 131-32, 136-37.

George Bishop and Co., for excerpts from A. Sandham, *Montreal, Past and Present* (Montreal, 1870), p. 216.

W. Bronson, author and editor of *Cry California*, for excerpts from "Ear Pollution," from the Fall, 1967 issue of *Cry California*, published by California Tomorrow, San Francisco.

Chateau de Ramezay and the author, for excerpts from L. M. Wilson, *This Was Montreal* (Montreal, 1960), p. 111.

Dial Press, for excerpts from James Baldwin, *Another Country* (New York, Dell, 1963), pp. 99-100.

Faber and Faber Ltd., for excerpts from E. Howard, *Garden Cities of Tomorrow* (London, 1946), p. 47.

Harcourt, Brace and World, Inc., for excerpts from L. Mumford, *The City in History* (New York, 1961), pp. 543-44.

H. M. H. Publishing Co. Inc. and R. Buckminster Fuller for excerpts from "City of the Future," *Playboy* (January, 1968), p. 166. Copyright © 1967 by H. M. H. Publishing Co. Inc.

Margaret Laurence and the *Vancouver Sun*, for the excerpt from "Love and Madness in the City," *Vancouver Sun* (November, 1969).

Lister and Co., for excerpts from City Council, *Hamilton, Canada* (Hamilton, 1913), pp. 95, 200.

The Observer (London, Eng.), for excerpts from J. Davy, "Poison Perils Our Planet," *The Observer* (November, 1968).

Penguin Books Ltd., for excerpts from U. Sinclair, *The Jungle* (Harmondsworth, 1965), pp. 30-31.

Queen's Printer, for excerpts from Economic Council of Canada, *Fifth Annual Review: The Challenge of Growth and Change* (Ottawa, 1968). Reproduced with the permission of the Queen's Printer for Canada.

Mordecai Richler, for excerpts from M. Richler, *Son of a Smaller Hero* (New York, 1965), pp. 13-14.

Schroder Music Co., for "Little Boxes," words and music by Malvina Reynolds. © copyright 1962 by Schroder Music Co. (ASCAP). Used by permission.

Stovel-Advocate Press Ltd., for excerpts from W. Healy, *Winnipeg's Early Days* (Winnipeg, 1927), p. 21.

Time Inc., for excerpts from "A Failure Everywhere," *Time* (September 12, 1969), and "Pierre Elliot Trudeau, Prime Minister," *Time* (October 17, 1969), Reprinted by permission from TIME, the Weekly Newsmagazine; Copyright Time Inc. 1969.

Thames and Hudson, for excerpts from A. Toynbee, *Cities of Destiny* (London, 1967), pp. 27-8.

Toronto Daily Star, for excerpts from J. Zaritsky, "Should the Great Road Be Finished or Stopped in its Tracks," *Toronto Daily Star* (November, 1969).

University of Toronto Press, for excerpts from H. Carver, *Cities in the Suburbs* (Toronto, 1962), pp. 12-13, 15, and 18. Reprinted by permission of the publishers. © University of Toronto Press, 1962.

Vancouver Province, for excerpts from "Town Spirit Won't Give Up Ghost," *Vancouver Province* (February, 1967).

Vancouver Sun, for excerpts from Reuter's News Agency Report, "President's Commission on Violence," *Vancouver Sun* (November, 1969).

Welbeck Music Ltd., London, Eng., for "Downtown," © copyright Welbeck Music Ltd.

Winnipeg Free Press, for excerpts from G. Elliot, *Winnipeg As It Is* (Winnipeg, 1874), pp. 15, 25-6.

Yale University Press, for excerpts from M. Katz, "Social Structure in Hamilton, Ontario," in S. Thernstrom and R. Sennett (eds.), *Nineteenth Century Cities* (New Haven, 1969), pp. 209-14.

Mr. Larry Hickman, for help in devising the exercise based on Fig. 6-13.

Dr. J. Lewis Robinson, for help in devising Fig. 2-14.